God's Treasure
RED SEA CROSSING

The Rabuns
Jer. 29: 11-14ᵈ
Dr. Pocahontas Schuck

DR. POCAHONTAS SCHUCK

WESTBOW
PRESS®
A DIVISION OF THOMAS NELSON
& ZONDERVAN

WestBow Press books may be ordered through booksellers or by contacting:

WestBow Press
A Division of Thomas Nelson & Zondervan
1663 Liberty Drive
Bloomington, IN 47403
www.westbowpress.com
1 (866) 928-1240

ISBN: 978-1-9736-9112-9 (sc)
ISBN: 978-1-9736-9113-6 (hc)
ISBN: 978-1-9736-9111-2 (e)

Library of Congress Control Number: 2020907781

Print information available on the last page.

WestBow Press rev. date: 05/27/2020

Contents

Charts and Maps

Charts

Maps

Illustrations

Introduction

In the past few years over time I observed articles that showed up online in reference to ancient wheels being discovered on the seafloor of bodies of water. I asked myself, could these really be the remains of an Egyptian army that drowned many years ago? I have read the account in the Bible and it seemed possible that these wheels could confirm or deny the incredible story.

Therefore I began searching in a methodical, organized manner for evidence that would point to the truth of this situation. The more I searched the more I was convinced that the evidence found by Ron Wyatt in 1978 in the Gulf of Aqaba did confirm what the Bible records in Exodus chapters 3-17.

Several sources online give detailed information about the discoveries of Ron Wyatt during the fourth quarter of the twentieth century. Primarily, these sources were anchorstone.com, arkdiscovery.com, biblebelievers.org.au, covenantkeepers.co.uk, discoveredsinai.com, nasa.com, truediscoveries.org, and ronwyatt.com. I also used an article from *Smithsonian* regarding the archaeological discoveries of Dr. Jodi Magness from the University of North Carolina Chapel Hill, an image from the CBS Morning News dated April 17, 1984, and a newsbreak from CBN Faithwire on October 17, 2019.

As you are reading my book, you may find material that you

have never thought to put together as I have. My thoughts ran in this direction due to the fact that I taught science (biology, chemistry, geology, general science, life science, and zoology) for more than forty-three years in public schools in Virginia, South Carolina, New Jersey, Connecticut, and Massachusetts. These ideas might give you food for thought and encourage you to look at the earth's history with a new perspective.

Acknowledgments

I am grateful to the following people who assisted me in this work: my pastor, Bishop Scottie Jackson, and Sister Darlene Jackson, for all of their patience in answering my myriad questions as I pursued my bachelor of biblical studies, my master of divinity, and my doctor of theology.

I am also grateful to Kitty, Aimee, Becky, Megan, Rita, Raechon, and Stephanie at the local Cooper Branch Library who faithfully guided me through the process of writing this paper. I also received help from Anne Barnes, Brenda Wendell, and Teresa Young.

My maternal grandmother, Sarah Virginia (Virgie) O'Dell Quesenberry planted seeds that sparked my interest in studying the Bible. When I was not even ten years old, she visited our home and mesmerized me with Bible stories as I sat at her feet. When I graduated from high school in 1959, she presented me with a white leatherette KJV Bible, which I still have and refer to even today.

CHAPTER 1
A Hypothesis

I BELIEVE THERE is abundant evidence in the Bible, written literature, and physical evidence to support the concept of the crossing of the Red Sea by Moses and the Israelites. A careful search of the maps in many Bibles in use today shows that Mt. Sinai, the Hebrews' destination, is located in the wrong country on the Sinai Peninsula—instead of in Saudi Arabia.

Map of Errors Found in the Back of Our Bibles

MAP of ERRORS found in the back of our BIBLES

Most of the place names on this map have never been located-despite 2,000 years of archaelogical expeditions. Their position can vary by 100 miles between different Bibles, often with a question mark after the name"?".

Archaeologists admit they do not know the true sites. The have not found the least evidence of their existence because they have been searching in the wrong locations. They have followed traditions based upon an arbitrary choice in the fourth century AD.

biblebelievers.org.au

1

This map confirms that archaeologists admit they do not know the true sites. The following quote gives a second supporting opinion that the "confusion over the Red Sea crossing stems from a wrong location for Mt. Sinai, which the Hebrews in actuality reached after crossing the Red Sea." According to *Ark Discovery* (2):

The traditional Mt. Sinai was "found" by Constantine's "psychic" mother, who in the fourth century, went around the Holy Land pointing out various sites as the "authentic" biblical sites.

The results of the lack of correct knowledge continue after the illustration. *True Discoveries* (20) clarifies the confusion by pointing out that the church began adopting these incorrect historic spots as the correct ones for biblical events. Therefore, many Christians have difficulty with the Red Sea crossing since the places on the land do not match the descriptions given in the biblical record. It is quite amazing that this error has continued until the present.

Stories have been concocted that the water was only a marsh, a couple of feet deep—and that this Exodus path went over the area of what is today the Suez Canal. It really would have been a miracle to drown Pharaoh's army (250,000 soldiers) in only two feet of water! As a result of all this confusion, there are people who still believe the Egyptian army drowned in the two-feet-deep marsh near the Suez Canal. Other people think that the Egyptians drowned in the lakes in the northern regions of the Gulf of Aqaba. If these people were aware of the huge numbers of Egyptian soldiers who drowned in the Gulf of Aqaba during the Exodus, according to Josephus, the Jewish historian, they would not—for even one minute—entertain the idea that they met their demise in a two-feet-deep marsh.

According to *True Discoveries* (21), Josephus wrote that the Egyptian army contained 250,000 soldiers.

Traditional Location for Mt. Sinai

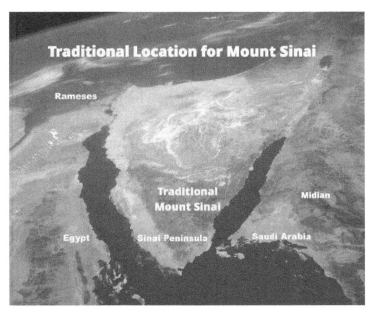

arkdiscovery.com

A nasa.gov photo shows the traditionally accepted positioning of Mt. Sinai on the Sinai Peninsula. My research will show the facts regarding the Red Sea Crossing, briefly discuss Mt. Sinai, and clarify that the Bible is truth. The Bible is the final word in understanding God's plan for freeing the Israelites from their bondage in Egypt. Another reference to the confusion surrounding the location of Mt. Sinai is illustrated in the following quote from an obviously confused person

In an article in *True Discoveries* (18), the author[1] states:

Hardly a place-name in the Bible's Exodus narrative can be fixed on Ark Discovery maps with any certainty... conjectures

---

[1] Arden, 1992, 420–46.

about Sinai's... unclear Biblical past—whether the route of the Exodus, the location of the "real" Mt. Sinai, or the origin of the pillar of fire—must be taken with a few grains—indeed, a dune—of desert sand.

Unfortunately, this person did not read the scripture in the New Testament, which states that the location of "Mt. Sinai (is) in Arabia" (Galatians 4:25). These references have clearly established—without any doubt—that there is great confusion regarding the location of Mt. Sinai, which is not located on the Sinai Peninsula. It is, however, located in northwestern Saudi Arabia, at a mountain named Jebel al-Lawz.

As background, Joseph, son of Jacob was sold for slavery in Egypt by his ten jealous brothers (Genesis 37:13-28). It is interesting to think about the relationship of the Egyptians and the Israelites (Hebrews). Initially, Joseph reigned as a vizier, the second-in-command in Egypt. The reigning king (the first pharaoh of our study) is believed to have been Djoser (*Anchor Stone*, 95). He invited Joseph's father, Jacob, and his entire family of seventy people plus livestock to live in the choice land of Goshen (Genesis 46:46-47).

Another amazing fact is that there were at least two times in history when Egyptian carts were used to transport the Israelites. The first use of carts was when Djoser ordered that carts be sent to Canaan to bring Joseph's father and family to Egypt to the land of Goshen (Genesis 46:5):

And Joseph placed his father and his brethren, and gave them a possession in the land of Egypt, in the best of the land, in the land of Rameses, as Pharaoh had commanded. (Genesis 47:11)

And Israel dwelt in the land of Egypt, in the country of Goshen; they had possessions therein, and grew, and multiplied exceedingly. (Genesis 47:27)

The second time that Egyptian carts and chariots were used to transport the Israelites was when Joseph's father, Israel, died. After his father's death, Joseph instructed his physicians to embalm Jacob (Israel) for forty days, following a period of mourning by the Egyptians for seventy days (Genesis 50:2–3). A very large number of Egyptian officials and dignitaries of the pharaoh's court accompanied Joseph and his relatives to Canaan. This was probably a different pharaoh because some references state that Djoser died in the fifth year of the famine. The purpose of the trip was to bury Israel and mourn another seven days in Canaan (Genesis 49:33–50:13).

Scripture does not tell us, but Egyptian carts may have been involved in the state funeral of Joseph after his death when he was 110 years old. This would have involved yet a different pharaoh. Joseph's body, at his request, was taken out of Egypt with the Israelites during the Exodus (Exodus 13:19). Do you suppose that some of these carts were destroyed in the Red Sea four hundred years later?

During the reign of yet another pharaoh, male Hebrew babies were slaughtered. Moses, a Hebrew baby, was saved by the pharaoh's daughter (Exodus 2:3–10). Many years later, the adult Moses had been training (co-regent) for approximately twenty-two years to become the next pharaoh in our story. He was, however, forced to leave Egypt because he killed an Egyptian who was abusing one of the Hebrew slaves (Exodus 2:12). He went to Midian and was exiled for forty years. Was this a coincidence or a *"God-incidence?"* Was God planning to train him to be a leader of the Israelites instead of a pharaoh for the Egyptians?

The key figure who is most associated with Mt. Sinai and the crossing of the Red Sea is Moses. In order to continue the saga of the true Mt. Sinai, we will go to find Moses living outside of Egypt (Exodus 2:15b-22) to protect his life from the pharaoh who wanted to kill him.

Moses had been living in Midian—in Saudi Arabia, near the mountain Jebel al-Lawz—for forty years since he murdered an Egyptian for beating a Hebrew man. He worked for his father-in-law, Jethro (Exodus 3:1). He married Zipporah, one of Jethro's daughters. They had two sons: Gershom and Eliezer (Exodus 18:3-4). One day, as Moses shepherded his father-in-law's sheep near Jebel al-Lawz, God spoke to him from a bush that burned but was not consumed (Exodus 3:1–2).

The following scriptures recount Moses's conversation with God speaking from a burning bush:

Now Moses kept the flock of Jethro his father in law, the priest of Midian: and he led the flock to the backside of the desert, and came to the mountain of God, even to Horeb. And the angel of the Lord appeared unto him in a flame of fire out of the midst of a bush: and he looked, and, behold, the bush burned with fire, and the bush was not consumed. And Moses said, I will now turn aside, and see this great sight, why the bush is not burnt. And when the Lord saw that he turned aside to see, God called unto him out of the midst of the bush, and said, Moses, Moses. And he said, Here am I. And he said, Draw not nigh hither: put off thy shoes from off thy feet, for the place whereon thou standest is holy ground. Moreover he said, I am the God of thy father, the God of Abraham, the God of Isaac, and the God of Jacob. And Moses hid his face; for he was afraid to look upon God. (Exodus 3:1–6)

And the Lord said, I have surely seen the affliction of my people which are in Egypt, and have heard their cry by reason of their taskmasters; for I know their sorrows; And I am come down to deliver them out of the hand of the Egyptians, and to bring them up out of that land unto a good land and a large, unto a land flowing with milk and honey; unto the place of the Canaanites, and the Hittites, and the Amorites, and the Perizzites, and the Hivites, and the Jebusites. Now therefore, behold, the cry of the children of Israel is come unto me: and I have also seen the oppression wherewith the Egyptians oppress them. Come now therefore, and I will send thee unto Pharaoh, that thou mayest bring forth my people the children of Israel out of Egypt. And Moses said unto God, Who am I, that I should go unto Pharaoh, and that I should bring forth the children of Israel out of Egypt? And he said, Certainly I will be with thee; and this shall be a token unto thee, that I have sent thee: When thou hast brought forth the people out of Egypt, ye shall serve God upon this mountain. And Moses said unto God, Behold, when I come unto the children of Israel, and shall say unto them, The God of your fathers hath sent me unto you; and they shall say to me, What is his name? what shall I say unto them? And God said unto Moses, I AM THAT I AM: and he said, Thus shalt thou say unto the children of Israel, I AM hath sent me unto you. (Exodus 3:7–14)

As I continued my reading, I wondered how the Egyptians and the Hebrews knew that God's name was I Am. Joseph's brothers sold him to a caravan headed for Egypt, and God later used the pharaoh to elevate Joseph to a position in Egypt that was second only to the pharaoh. In my research (*Anchor Stone*, 3), I found that Joseph's name was Imhotep. Therefore, the Egyptians and the Hebrews had been familiar with God speaking to them through Joseph. He was also known to them as Imhotep ("I am Hotep.").

Step Pyramid Located in Saqqara

arkdiscovery.com

In the third dynasty, Imhotep was the designer of the step pyramid in Saqqara, which was the burial tomb for Djoser. This pyramid may have been one of the structures used by Joseph to store grain for the following seven years of famine. Research seems to show that Joseph's grain distribution was a major factor in Egypt becoming a wealthier nation.

After his conversation with God on the mountain, Moses spoke to his father-in-law. Jethro gave him permission to return to Egypt with his wife, Zipporah, and their two sons, Gershom and Eliezer. (Exodus 4:18-20)

And Moses went and returned to Jethro his father in law, and said unto him, Let me go, I pray thee, and return unto my brethren which are in Egypt, and see whether they be yet alive. And Jethro said to Moses, Go in peace. And the Lord said unto Moses in Midian, Go, return into Egypt: for all the men are dead which sought thy life. And Moses took his wife and his sons, and set them upon an ass, and he returned to the land of Egypt: and Moses took the rod of God in his hand.

When Moses returned to Egypt, he and his brother Aaron, a priest from the tribe of Levi, spoke to Pharaoh many times and urged him to let the Israelites go to the wilderness to worship God (Exodus 4:5-10).

The following chart summarizes the ten plagues that God sent to the Egyptians because Pharaoh refused to let the Hebrews go. This chart compares the plagues that occurred in Egypt with the future events that are explained in the book of Revelation. These events are still scheduled to occur on earth in the last days. Learning about these events, which really happened on earth in the past, is a reality check. They are not fables or myths, and they are certainly not designed as entertainment.

These plagues actually did occur, which the chart shows. If similar events are scheduled by God, it would make sense for everyone to be aware of them and make preparations to be spared as the Israelites were during the plagues. Many people walk around absorbed in their daily lives—their successes and struggles—but they are totally unaware of these future events that God has scheduled. This chart presents the eye-opening series of catastrophes that are planned for our planet.

The Plagues of Egypt in Exodus Compared to Future Events in Revelation

Ex 7:17	Waters in the river turn to blood	Rev 8:8	Third of sea became blood
		Rev 11:6	2 witness turn water to blood
		Rev 16:4	Waters became blood
Ex 8:5	Frogs go from water to land	Rev 16:13	3 spirits of devils like frogs
Ex 9:10	Boils on man and beast	Rev 16:2	Sores on men w. Beast mark
Ex 9:24	Thunder, hail, and Fire	Rev 8:5	Thunder, and lightning
		Rev 8:7	Hail & fire mixed with blood
		Rev 16:21	Hailstones weighing 75 lbs.
Ex 10:15	Locusts covered the earth	Rev 9:3	Smoke locust to hurt men
Ex 10:22	Darkness in Egypt 3 days	Rev 8:12	Third of sun, moon, stars dark
		Rev 16:10	Beast kingdom in darkness
Ex 12:29	Death of the firstborn in Egypt	Rev 9:18	Third of men killed

As I searched for the truth of the Red Sea crossing and the plagues in Egypt, I discovered a lack of Egyptian historical references around that time in history. Some people seem to think the Egyptians did not keep any records if they were not in a favorable position. However, I was amazed that I was able to find documented history of what appear to be eyewitness accounts of the plagues in an ancient Egyptian document (*True Discoveries*, 34) that mirror the facts found in the Bible.

There is an ancient Egyptian papyrus document called the Ipuwer Papyrus, which seems to recount in eye-witness fashion the plague of blood, the plague of cattle, the plague of strange fire, the plague on the firstborn, as well as the strange darkness—events previously known only from the Bible, in the Book of Exodus. The *Ipuwer Papyrus*, often referred to as the *Papyrus Ipuwer*, is believed to have been written between 1600 BC and 1850 BC. The oldest copy in existence was purchased from a collector in 1828 and translated into English in 1909.

Currently, the *Ipuwer Papyrus* resides in the Dutch National Museum of Antiquities in Leiden, Netherlands.

This small piece of papyrus has sparked a great deal of debate, and scholars remain divided on its true meaning and purpose. The primary interest for our purposes is the striking similarities to the plagues recorded in the book of Exodus. First, let's take a look at the similarities between the *Ipuwer Papyrus* and the book of Exodus. There is no denying the two are shockingly similar, and it should come as no surprise that many use the papyrus in their arguments for the story of the plagues being historical fact.

1. Exodus 7:20: "And all the waters that were in the river were turned to blood."
   Ipuwer: "The river is blood"
2. Exodus 7:24: "And all the Egyptians digged round about the river for water to drink, for they could not drink of the water of the river."
   Ipuwer: "Men… thirst after water."
3. Exodus 9:23: "... and fire ran along upon the ground."
   Ipuwer: "Gates, columns and walls are consumed by fire."
4. Exodus 9:31: "And the flax and the barley was smitten: for the barley was in the ear."
   Ipuwer: "Everywhere barley has perished."
5. Exodus 9:3: " ...upon the horses, upon the asses, upon the camels, upon the oxen, and upon the sheep: there shall be a very grievous murrain."
   Ipuwer: "The cattle moan because of the state of the land."
6. Exodus 12:29: "... the Lord smote all the firstborn in the land of Egypt."

Ipuwer: "Men are few, and he who places his brother in the land is everywhere. The children of princes are dashed against the walls."

7. Exodus 10:22: "And Moses stretched forth his hand toward heaven, and there was a thick darkness in all the land of Egypt three days."

   Ipuwer: "The land was not light or bright."

8. Exodus 12:35: "... the children of Israel... borrowed of the Egyptians jewels of silver, and jewels of gold, and raiment"

   Ipuwer: "Gold, lapis lazuli, silver are strung on the necks of maidservants."

The Ipuwer also speaks of a pestilence throughout the land of Egypt and the collapse of civil order; servants were leaving their servitude and acting rebelliously. Some translations tell how the king was taken away by poor men. Writings taken from Egyptian antiquities appear to suggest that the Egyptians didn't keep written records when they were losing. However, other writings seem to recount a grim situation after the loss of possibly as many as 550,000 men in the Red Sea crossing. Still other writings record information that the servant or slave population was greatly reduced. This is easy to understand since they lost six hundred thousand Hebrew servants. Some seem to suggest that although the Egyptians tried to keep the devastating loss from becoming widely known, there were invasions of foreign powers during this time.

After the ninth plague, God told Moses and Aaron about the guidelines and restrictions for the Feast of Unleavened Bread and Passover (Exodus 12:1–20; 12:43–51). The Israelites were in their homes in Goshen. That day, they killed the lamb and spread the blood on the top and both sides of the doorframe.

Then they observed their Passover meal and made preparations for their exit. The people bowed down and worshipped. The Israelites did just what the Lord commanded Moses and Aaron to do. At midnight, the Lord sent the death angel throughout the land of Egypt to slay the firstborn in the homes of the greatest to the least and even the firstborn of their livestock (Exodus 12:21–30).

The Israelites, having placed the blood on the doorframes of their homes, survived the death of the firstborn of all their people and their livestock. They were spared the loss that the Egyptians experienced. However, little did they know what lay ahead of them on their journey to the Promised Land.

The image below shows what they endured on their journey with Moses, their leader. In the center of the NASA image the terrain is filled with massive mountains. Only a pathway winds its way through this otherwise impassable terrain. The local people call this the Wadi Watir, and it will become their way to "freedom" as they exit onto a very large beach.

Wadi Watir-Nuweiba Beach-Gulf of Aqaba

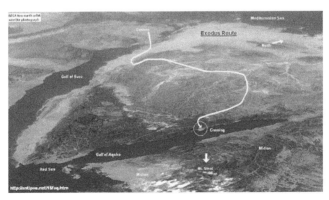

nasa.com

CHAPTER 2
The Israelites Leave Goshen

Route of the Hebrews from Egypt to Mt. Sinai

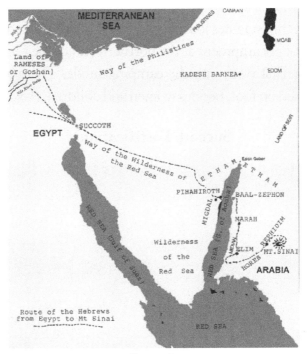

truediscoveries.org

FINALLY, PHARAOH SUMMONED Moses and Aaron in the night with clear instructions that they and their livestock were to leave Egypt immediately (Exodus 12:31–33). As the departure was being realized, the Egyptians freely complied with requests for gifts of gold, silver, and clothing for the Israelites (Exodus 12:35–36). The Israelites had been in Egypt for exactly 430 years to the day (Exodus 12:40–41).

When Pharaoh told the people that they were allowed to leave (the day after the angel of death visited Egypt), they all left their homes in the Nile Delta area. This area was also called the land of Rameses or Goshen (see previous map). They proceeded to leave Egypt proper. Once the Israelites reached Succoth, they were no longer in Egypt (Exodus 13:20). There was a city called Rameses (Exodus 1:11), but it was distinct from the land of Rameses. Rameses was the land given to Joseph's family to live in by the Pharaoh:

Firstly, the Israelites journeyed from Rameses to Succoth. This was the first encampment at the northern end of the Gulf of Suez, where they first went into the camping mode. There were about 600,000 men on foot, besides women and children. (Exodus 12:37)

Succoth Fortifications

truediscoveries.org

This chart (*True Discoveries*, 17) explains how approximately two million people were included in the Exodus from Egypt to Sinai under the leadership of Moses.

Calculations of the Total Number of Israelites

Table 8. The numbers refer to fighting men over the age of 20 years two years after the crossing of the Red Sea and shown according to the tribe to which they belonged (Numb. 1:17-50).

Tribe	Number
Reuben	46 500
Simeon	59 300
Gad	45 560
Judah	74 600
Issachar	54 400
Zebulun	57 400
Joseph	40 500
Manasseh	32 200
Benjamin	35 400
Dan	62 700
Asher	41 500
Naphtali	53 400
Total	603 550

Table 10. Calculation of the total number of people based on the population census of fighting men two years after the Exodus (Numb. 1:17-50, 3:14-39).

Fighting men	603 550
Equal number of women	603 550
Under 20 years old	321 900
Over 60 years old	241 400
Levite men	22 300
Equal number of Levite women	22 300
Total number of Hebrews	1 815 000
A "mixed multitude"(assuming that they were 10% of the Hebrew population)	181 000
Total number	1 996 000

truediscoveries.org

Some people have questioned how they could leave Egypt so quickly. Ron Wyatt (2–3) pointed out that Egypt is very long but its east-west boundaries are very narrow. At times, the Sinai Peninsula was part of Egypt, and at other times, it was controlled by Israel. The statement that they were "now out of Egypt" means they were out of the main part of Egypt. As the next map shows, Egypt proper is west of the Suez Canal. They had left Egypt proper once they crossed the line of fortification—just as the Lord had promised.

A broad canal connected the lakes of the isthmus and a fortress of T'aru (also called Tharu and Takut). Moses was well acquainted with Tharu (called Succoth in the Bible). Tharu was the area where Egyptian military expeditions were organized. The Egyptian army consisted of a large number of men, horses, and chariots. They would soon be drowned on the floor of the Red Sea. "And Moses was learned in all the wisdom of the Egyptians, and was mighty in words and in deeds" (Acts 7:22-42). 'Stephen's summary of the Exodus'

Since he had been raised by Pharaoh's daughter and trained in the military and in the priesthood of Egypt, they intended for him to be the successor to his Egyptian stepmother's father. *True Discoveries* (10) states that it seems to have been a well-known fact that Moses was a general in the Egyptian army.

Josephus (AD 93–94) wrote that "as a military man, once again, Moses knew 'Tharu,' and it was here that he organized his largest 'army' to ever travel."

Not only had God provided a leader (Moses) trained in this area but He had also provided a huge space for the 'Israelites to be arranged in an orderly fashion by Moses for their journey to the mountain of God.

"And the children of Israel went up harnessed out of the land of Egypt" (Exodus 13:18). "The term *harassed* comes from a Hebrew word *chamushim*, which means "in ranks." Therefore, the Israelites were not a fleeing mob but an organized unit. And from this assembly point, they traveled to Etham" (*True Discoveries*, 4).

Nuwayba' al Muzayyinah

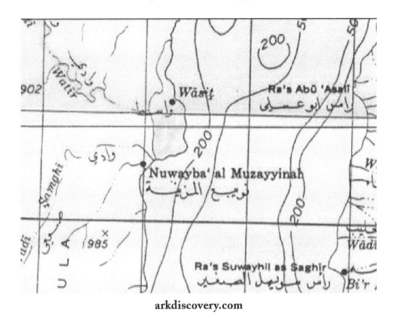

The Route of the Exodus

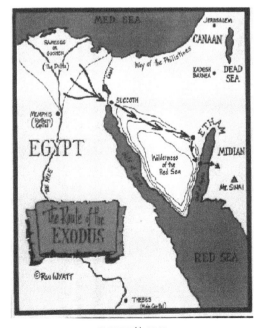

CHAPTER 3

Travel through Etham and Wadi Watir to Nuweiba

THE WILDERNESS OF the Red Sea was the mountainous land of the middle and southern Sinai Peninsula.

When Pharaoh let the people go, God did not lead them on the road through the Philistine country, though that was shorter. For God said, "If they face war, they might change their minds and return to Egypt." So God led the people around by the desert road toward the Red Sea. (Exodus 13:17–18)

According to *True Discoveries* (10), this well-known route was and had been used in the past by caravans and the army. It was safer than along the coast where they might encounter the Philistines.

And they took their journey from Succoth, and encamped in Etham, in the edge of the wilderness. And the Lord went before them by day in a pillar of a cloud, to lead them the way; and by night in a pillar of fire, to give them light; to go by day and night: He took not away the pillar of the cloud by day, nor the pillar of fire by night, from before the people. (Exodus 13:20–22)

The pillars of the Lord are clearly the work of the third part

21

of the Trinity, the Holy Spirit, who led them to Etham (see map on previous page). According to *True Discoveries* (20), the land was located around the mid-northern edge of the gulf of Aqaba. Ron Wyatt, believed that once they crossed the Red Sea, they were still in Etham. The Israelites probably traveled at night as well as during the day to get as much distance between them and the Egyptians as possible. Exodus 13:22 points out that the cloud by day and fire by night means that the Holy Spirit was in continual operation since the Israelites were in constant movement.

Wadi Watir and Nuweiba Beach

ronwyatt.com

The Israelites entered the mountains along a dry riverbed system that must have appeared like an endless maze to them. The twenty-seven-kilometer (seventeen-mile) Wadi Watir is a natural highway from Egypt. The multitude comprised 603,000 men—as well as women and children—perhaps as many as two million people (see previous chart). As the great multitude weaved its way through the awesome and wild canyon, it would appear that they were entangled. Hemmed in to the left and right, they could travel in only one direction. The only path through that particular wadi leads to an enormous beach, which is so big that it can be seen on Google Earth satellite photos (images available online). According to *Covenant Keepers* (1), after researching the route the Israelites took in their exodus from Egypt, Ron Wyatt found that the biblical description fit perfectly with a deep gorge called Wadi Watir. In Exodus 14:1–2, God told them to turn off the highway, which Wyatt (4) found led to the canyon Wadi Watir.

The Bible records the reaction of Pharaoh when he was informed of their deviation from the highway: "They are entangled in the land, the wilderness hath shut them in" (Exodus 14:3). Wadi Watir is a long, deep canyon that perfectly fits the description of a wilderness. The Israelites changed from a northerly direction, which would have taken them around the northern tip of Aqaba at Etham.

A question arises as to whether the Gulf of Aqaba was too far away from Goshen for the children of Israel to get there within a week. The Bible says that they traveled both day and night (Exodus 13:21). A clue comes to mind. The bread they were eating was unleavened. They ate unleavened bread because they were traveling and did not have time to let the bread rise. The prescribed amount of time for the eating of unleavened bread was seven days—the same number of days required to get from their home in Goshen, in Egypt, to the Gulf of Aqaba to cross the Red Sea. Moses knew that the Egyptians would spend time burying their dead and mourning their losses after the tenth plague, but he also knew that they would be seeking revenge. Therefore, Moses had to get his two million people moving quickly.

The journey from Succoth to the Red Sea in this short time span suggests a miracle. *True Discoveries* (17) points out that it was not a short trip to the Gulf of Aqaba as tradition states; however it would have been shorter to the Gulf of Suez. Instead, it was a huge endeavor. Moving several hundred people would have been difficult enough, but they had to move two million people—including infants and the elderly—livestock, and perhaps even baby animals. This had to constitute a miracle. It could not have been accomplished with their own strength.

The scripture confirms other miracles:

Ye have seen what I did unto the Egyptians, and how I bare you on eagles' wings, and brought you unto myself. (Exodus 19:4)

When the Bible refers to eagles, it usually means being swift "The first was like a lion, and had eagle's wings" (Daniel 7:4). This lion is Alexander, and it refers to the speed with which he took over the empire. Scripture also refers to another miraculous event. God's servant, Moses, spent forty years in the wilderness:

And I have led you forty years in the wilderness: your clothes are not waxen old upon you, and thy shoe is not waxen old upon thy foot. (Deuteronomy 29:5)

Other examples in the scriptures illustrate this point:

- "a nation as swift as the eagle" (Deuteronomy 28:49)
- "as the eagle that hasteth" (Job 9:26)
- "were swifter than eagles" (2 Samuel 1:23)
- "are swifter than eagles" (Jeremiah 4:13)
- "swifter than eagles" (Lamentations 4:19)

Looking at this travel distance logically, is it possible to cover this amount of space within days and nights? *True Discoveries* (18) compares the Israelites traveling through the wilderness to a more recent journey. The distance from the Gulf of Suez to Nuweiba is 210 miles (336 kilometers). In 1967, the Israeli troops, under Moshe Dayan, marched this same route—in reverse from Nuweiba to Succoth—in six days, stopping at night to camp. The average speed of the Israeli troops was 2.9 miles (4.67 kilometers) per hour. Using this information, it was definitely possible for the Israelites to have traveled to the huge beach, Nuweiba, within seven days.

Red Sea Crossing

arkdiscovery.com

Today, the beach is called "Nuweiba." The full name is Nuwayba al Muzayyinah, which means "waters of Moses opening" (*Ark Discovery*, 17–18). According to the Arabic-English Dictionary, the root of this name suggests that a misfortunate incident happened there. According to *Ark Discovery* (6), it is speculative to say whether or not the misfortunate incident refers to the drowning of the Egyptian army in the Red Sea. Others say it was the typical custom of the people of that time to name a place after an attribute of the local geology.

Pi-Hahiroth is located above where the Wadi Watir joins the Nuweiba Beach. Pi-Hahiroth means "mouth of gorges" (*Strong's Concordance*). Below is a relatively up-to-date photo of the end of the road where the Israelites first laid eyes on the impasse existing between them and freedom

Wadi Watir and Highway

truediscoveries.org

At the end of the highway, the Wadi Watir and the Red Sea (Gulf of Aqaba) can be seen. It would be hard to imagine how discouraged the tired, hungry Israelites felt when they saw the Red Sea. For they had been traveling on foot for seven days, eating unleavened bread, and carrying their bundles. And then they looked ahead and saw that the Wadi Watir led to a wide expanse of beach on the Gulf of Aqaba.

This beach at Nuweiba is so large, it could easily have held the multitude, their flocks, and Pharaoh's pursuing army. There would have even been room for several kilometers to separate the two groups. The size of this beach is seven by three kilometers

(4.35 miles by 1.9 miles). It is so large that it can easily be seen on Google Earth satellite photos (images available online). It is the only place that matches all the requirements of our checklist and the Bible: "They are entangled in the land, the wilderness hath shut them in" (Exodus 14:3).

Confirmation is added by Josephus (book II, chapter xv) that the Hebrews were shut up:

Between the inaccessible cliffs and the sea; for there was (on each side) a range of mountains that terminated at the sea, which was impassable by reason of their roughness, and obstructed their flight where (the ridges of) the mountains were closed with the sea.

There was a migdol, an Egyptian military fortress, on the north end of the beach. According to Ron Wyatt (5), the ancient fortress prevented them from going north when they entered the beach area. The following photo shows the beautiful, inviting oasis.

Migdol: Egyptian Military Fortress

arkdiscovery.com

This photograph makes the following scripture easier to understand:

Speak unto the children of Israel, that they turn and encamp before Pi-Hahiroth, between Migdol and the sea, over against Baal-zephon: before it shall ye encamp by the sea. (Exodus 14:2)

According to *Ark Discoveries,* a migdol was an Egyptian military fortress (5). There is a lot of disagreement in the research as to the meaning of the words Pi-Hahiroth and migdol. However, it makes sense to me that Pi-Hahiroth is the opening from the Wadi Watir (canyon) to Nuweiba, the huge beach, and that the migdol is the fortress on the beach.

The migdol was the ancient fort on the narrowest point on the beach, and the gulf and the mountains were in close proximity (*Covenant Keepers,* 2). The fortress blocked any northern escape route along the beach. When arriving at the beach where the crossing took place, the children of Israel felt trapped. They could not turn back or head north because of the three-story Egyptian military fortress at the northern end of the beach. It is still standing today and is undergoing restoration. Today, you will find many hotels and a village along this five-mile stretch of beach.

According to the Bible, the Israelites were to encamp by the sea, directly opposite Baal-zephon (Exodus 14:2). On the opposite shore, in Saudi Arabia, precisely across from where they camped by the sea, is another ancient structure. All alone on the beach, it may have been a Midianite fortress, dedicated to Baal. I believe this could be Baal-zephon (Exodus 14:1–2). Because Baal-zephon was considered a protector of maritime trade, his Canaanite and Phoenician devotees constructed sanctuaries in his honor around the Mediterranean. Baal-zephon thereby also became a place-name, most notably a location mentioned in the book of Exodus as the location where the Israelites miraculously crossed the Red Sea during their exodus from Egypt.

In rabbinical literature, the idol at Baal-zephon was the only one that remained unharmed when God sent the tenth plague upon Egypt. The tenth plague brought death to men and animals and destroyed the idols. When Pharaoh overtook Israel at the sea, near Baal-zephon (Exodus 14:9), he said, "This idol, Baal-zephon, is indeed mighty, and the God of Israel is powerless over him." It is believed that God intentionally spared Baal-zephon in order to strengthen the infatuation of the wicked Pharaoh (Jewish Encyclopedia). According to Dr. Kyle McCarter of Johns Hopkins University and Dr. James Hoffmeier of Wheaton College, Baal-zephon is believed to be a coastal mountain. Some sources suggest it to be Mount Tiran.

Baalzephon

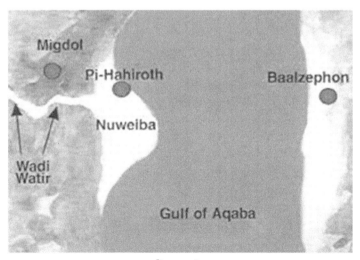

truediscoveries.org

29

CHAPTER 4
Red Sea Crossing

Gulf of Aqaba (Red Sea)

arkdiscovery.com

THE RED SEA crossing of the Israelites from their captivity and slavery in Egypt is very much a documented and valid reality. However, in the twenty-first century, a large number of people totally discount this miraculous event and think the Old Testament is being old-fashioned and outdated. Some of these people *say* they are Christians. How could anyone profess to be a Christian or follower of Christ and discount the firm foundation given to us in the Word of God expressed in the Old Testament? Jesus, God Himself, quoted the scriptures in the Old Testament seventy-five times. He quoted from the Torah (the first five books) twenty-six times.

The following documentation clarifies beyond any doubt that the Red Sea Crossing of the Israelites occurred, and it shows the exact part of the Red Sea where the crossing took place. This documentation confirms that the true Mt. Sinai is located in Saudi Arabia and not in Egypt as many modern Bible maps show. Nuweiba Beach was large enough to hold all the people. Documentation shows that two million people from Goshen would have been present when the army of 250,000 Egyptians caught up with the fleeing Hebrews. All of this happened the night before the crossing. It is amazing that traditional landmarks have prevailed over facts.

And it was told the King of Egypt that the people fled: and the heart of Pharaoh and of his servants was turned against the people, and they said, Why have we done this, that we have let Israel go from serving us? And he made ready his chariot, and took his people with him: And he took six-hundred chosen chariots, and all the chariots of Egypt, and captains over every one of them. (Exodus 14:5–7)

Of course, the Israelites could not turn around and retrace their steps because the Egyptian army was pursuing them. God had brought them to a point where only He could deliver them.

And when Pharaoh drew nigh, the children of Israel lifted up their eyes, and, behold, the Egyptians marched after them; and they were sore afraid: and the children of Israel cried out unto the Lord. And they said unto Moses, Because there were no graves in Egypt, hast thou taken us away to die in the wilderness? wherefore hast thou dealt thus with us, to carry us forth out of Egypt? Is not this the word that we did tell thee in Egypt, saying, Let us alone, that we may serve the Egyptians? For it had been better for us to serve the Egyptians, than that we should die in the wilderness. (Exodus 14:10–12)

The descendants of Jacob had been traveling for days and eating unleavened bread since there was no time to let the bread rise. Centuries later, many of the Jewish people (Israelites or Hebrews) still annually observe this festival for seven days. The Hebrews were about to witness the greatest deliverance in the history of the planet besides the deliverance from death of Jesus 1,446 years later.

"And Moses said unto the people, Fear ye not, *stand still*, and see the *salvation* of the Lord" (Exodus 14:13). The New Testament includes instructions for putting on the armor of God (Ephesians 6:10–18). Believers are to *stand*—not fight—and believe that God will fight for them. Ephesians 6:17 also mentions *salvation*.

And Moses said unto the people, fear ye not, *stand still* and see the *salvation* of the Lord which he will shew to you today. For the Egyptians whom ye have seen today, ye shall see them again no more forever. The Egyptians you see today, you will never see again. The Lord shall fight for you, and ye shall hold your peace" (be still). (Exodus 14:13–14)

One of the hardest things a Christian is asked to do is to stand still when all hope seems gone and the world appears to be crumbling around them. The normal path in dealing with difficult situations would seem to be to put together all our strength and make our own pitiful attempt to resolve the issue. However, we have an example to follow in Daniel. When he was cast into the den of lions, his best strategy was to *stand and trust* God to shut the mouths of the lions.

Then the king arose very early in the morning, and went in

33

haste unto the den of lions. And when he came to the den, he cried with a lamentable voice unto Daniel: and the king spake and said to Daniel, O Daniel, servant of the living God, is thy God, whom thou servest continually, able to deliver thee from the lions? Then said Daniel unto the king, O king, live forever. My God hath sent his angel, and hath shut the lions' mouths, that they have not hurt me: forasmuch as before him innocency was found in me; and also before thee, O king, have I done no hurt. (Daniel 6:19–22)

Model: Gulf of Aqaba

truediscoveries.org

It certainly is not surprising that God engineered this land bridge for the Israelites to use when they needed a path across the Gulf of Aqaba. God is not bound by time because He is not confined to earth. He was in control of the formation of the land bridge. In Junior high Earth Science class we learned that time exists because of the rotation of the earth (giving us day and night) and the revolution around the sun (which gives us our years). God, being outside and above time, knew that the Israelites would need a pathway in the future. Therefore, God formed the land bridge during the chaotic time of Noah's Flood.

True Discoveries (23) explains the Aqaba Crossing in the

following terms: "without taking the land bridge into account, some wonder whether the Gulf of Aqaba is too deep to cross." With the number of feet in a mile being 5,280, it is clear that the following measurements are close to a mile. Depth measurements for the Eilat (Elate) Deep are recorded as five thousand feet, and the Argonne (Aragonese) Deep as six thousand feet. Precisely and miraculously placed between these depths is the eight-to-nine-mile land bridge. Eilat Deep is north of the crossing almost at the tip of Aqaba, and Argonne is only slightly south of the crossing. The entrance is conveniently placed at Nuweiba Beach, which is large enough to hold the two million Israelites and Pharaoh's army.

On the opposite shore, in Saudi Arabia, the canyon area was large enough to hold the entire Israeli group. On the Egyptian side, the slope of the land bridge is a gentle six degrees for approximately three hundred feet. It gradually rises to exit on the Saudi shoreline. With this length and slope, amazingly there would have been no perceptible fall or rise to the Hebrews walking on the dry land.

The data for the depth was based on the ETOP05 database and is claimed to be a combination from various databases. It must be pointed out that there is a lot of disagreement among the various sources regarding the true depth of many of the areas in question. Basically, what is not in question is the seemingly shallowness of the land bridge and the two deeps on either side which are approximately a mile deep. Some people have compared these deeps to our own Grand Canyon in Arizona.

True Discoveries (23) explains the formation of the land bridge as two washouts meeting each other from two different directions as Almighty God formed the land bridge during the last phases of Noah's Flood in order to provide this "road to freedom" for the Israelites.

Admiralty Chart 756 (1952)

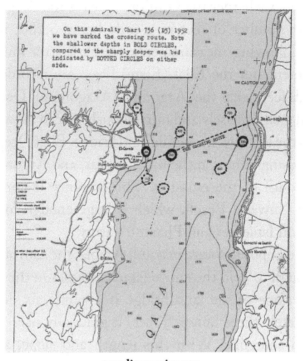

truediscoveries.org

Scriptures (KJV) refer to the Creator making a:

- "the *great deep*" (Isaiah 51:10)
- "the *mighty waters*" (Isaiah 43:16–17)
- "the *deep*" (Isaiah 63:11–13)
- "the *depths* have covered them" (Exodus 15:5)
- "the *depths* were congealed in the *heart of the sea*" (Exodus 15:8)
- "into the *deeps*" (Nehemiah 9:11)

God, of course, did not bring the Hebrews out of Goshen, His chosen land for them for 430 years, to have them pounded to dust on the beach, Nuweiba, by the Egyptian horde. With venom in their breath, they were eager to annihilate the Israelites, but God sent His Holy Spirit in the cloud to intervene.

And the Angel of God, which went before the camp of Israel, removed and went behind them; and the pillar of the cloud went from before their face, and stood behind them: And it came between the camp of the Egyptians and the camp of Israel; and it was a cloud and darkness to them, but it gave light by night to these: so that the one came not near the other all the night. (Exodus 14:19–20)

Did Moses, as he was trying to figure out his next step in a plan of action, lean on and remember God's Word to him in Exodus 3:12b? "When thou hast brought forth the people out of Egypt, ye shall serve God upon this mountain." The biblical text is not totally clear, but did Moses freak out? When Moses was all alone with God on Mt. Sinai, he probably had a totally different perspective as to the challenges facing him then than he did now. At that time he was having a peaceful conversation with God; now he is up against a sea of water on one side and an angry mob of two million people on the other side.

And the Lord said unto Moses, Wherefore criest thou unto me? speak unto the children of Israel, that they go forward: But lift thou up thy rod, and stretch out thine hand over the sea, and divide it: and the children of Israel shall go on dry ground through the midst of the sea. And I, behold, I will harden the hearts of the Egyptians, and they shall follow them: and I will get me honour upon Pharaoh, and upon all his host, upon his chariots, and upon his horsemen. And the Egyptians shall know that I am the Lord, when I have gotten me honour upon Pharaoh, upon his chariots, and upon his horsemen. (Exodus 14:15–18)

Moses Stretched Out His Hand

arkdiscovery.com

And Moses stretched out his hand over the sea; and the Lord caused the sea to go back by a strong east wind all that night, and made the sea dry land, and the waters were divided. And the children of Israel went into the midst of the sea upon the dry ground: and the waters were a wall unto them on their right hand, and on their left. But the children of Israel walked upon dry land in the midst of the sea. Thus the Lord saved Israel that day out of the hand of the Egyptians. (Exodus 14:21–22, 29a, 30a, 31)

And the Egyptians pursued, and went in after them to the midst of the sea, even all Pharaoh's horses, his chariots, and his horsemen. And it came to pass, that in the morning watch the Lord looked unto the host of the Egyptians through the pillar of fire and of the cloud, and troubled the host of the Egyptians, And took off their chariot wheels, that they drave them heavily: so that the Egyptians said, Let us flee from the face of Israel; for the Lord fighteth for them against the Egyptians. And the Lord said unto Moses, Stretch out thine hand over the sea, that the waters may come again upon the Egyptians, upon their chariots, and upon their horsemen. And Moses stretched forth his hand over the sea, and the sea returned to his strength when the morning appeared; and the Egyptians fled against it and the Lord overthrew the Egyptians in the midst of the sea. (Exodus 14:23-27)

Egyptian Chariots Graveyard

truediscoveries.org

And the waters returned, and covered the chariots, and the horsemen, and all the host of Pharaoh that came into the sea after them; there remained not so much as one of them. But the children of Israel walked upon dry land in the midst of the sea; and the waters were a wall unto them on their right hand, and on their left. Thus the Lord saved Israel that day out of the hand of the Egyptians; and Israel saw the Egyptians dead upon the sea shore. And Israel saw that great work which the Lord did upon the Egyptians: and the people feared the Lord, and believed the Lord, and his servant Moses. (Exodus 14:28–31)

In 1978, Ron Wyatt (ronwyatt.com) and his two sons, Daniel and Ronald Jr., were the first—or definitely among the first—to discover the coral-encrusted Egyptian artifacts strewn along the bottom of the land bridge connecting Egypt to Saudi

Arabia in the Gulf of Aqaba. Many people had unsuccessfully tried to locate these treasures over the centuries. So how did Ron Wyatt manage to be so successful? He was successful because he studied the scriptures; he had carefully planned and paid close attention to the details in the Bible. Some people say he also used his Walmart fish-finder to help locate the depth and location of the land bridge in order to search for the remains of the Egyptian army.

At first, it was difficult for Wyatt and his sons to discern what was natural coral and what was sea life (see photo). Also it was hard to see what remained of the chariot wheels left by the Egyptian army. According to Josephus, there were 250,000 men from Egypt; all of the Egyptians who entered the Gulf of Aqaba drowned there. The enhanced photo makes it easier to see the actual coral-covered wheel. As their eyes adjusted, they were amazed at the large number of wheels they found. Ron Wyatt took many photos of the artifacts on the seafloor of the Gulf of Aqaba in the late seventies and early eighties.

Actual Coral-Covered Chariot Wheel
Shape of Wheel - enhanced image

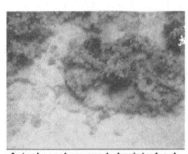 

Actual coral covered chariot wheel   Shape of wheel -- enhanced image

anchorstone.com   anchorstone.com

Of the four-, six-, and eight-spoked wheels that Ron

discovered, he retrieved an eight-spoked chariot wheel, which he took to the director of Egyptian antiquities, Dr. Nassif Mohammed Hassen, for verification. It was verified to have come from the Eighteenth Dynasty of Egypt. Since then, many other individuals and groups have explored this area. One of these divers, Viveka Ponten, lived in Saudi Arabia until the 1990s. She explored the Saudi Arabian side and took many photographs.

Two Wheels Still Attached to Axles

anchorstone.com   anchorstone.com

Mr. Wyatt made the astute observation that these marine organisms were probably the agents the Lord used to preserve the chariot wheels. If the exodus occurred, as many believe, in 1446 BC, then these artifacts have been resting in the Red Sea (Aqaba) for the past 3,465 years.

Other finds (*Covenant Keepers*, 3) include a human rib cage, a horse's hoof, and a coralized (not petrified but replaced by coral) right human femur of a 162-centimeter (five-foot-four) man. Aaron Sen and Dr. Nerida Titchiner stated that they found the coralized bone in a large pile of similar coralized bones. The coralized bone was taken to and verified by Professor Lennart Moller of the Department of Osteology at Stockholm University. His book, *The Exodus*

Case, provides a very extensive look at the details surrounding this subject. Several other excellent resources are *The Exodus Revealed* by Discovery Media, *The Exodus Conspiracy,* and recently released *The Red Sea Crossing* by Mahoney Media. This well done two and a half hour movie was shown throughout the United States for one day only on February 18, 2020. *The Red Sea Crossing Part II* also by Mahoney Media will be shown on May 5, 2020.

Human Rib Cage

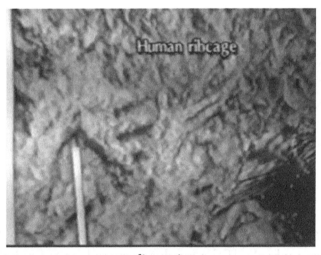

truesdiscoveries.org

Horse's Hoof

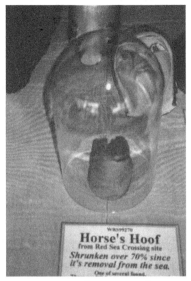

covenantkeepers.co.uk

Human Femur

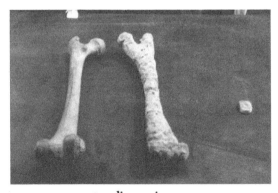

truediscoveries.org

These photos taken on the Egyptian side confirm that the Egyptian army entered the Gulf of Aqaba at this point. Ron found a gold chariot wheel, which he believed came from the chariot of a priest. The wood of the four-spoked gold chariot wheel deteriorated long ago, which left the specimen very fragile.

Moving the artifact most likely would have destroyed it. The wheel was discovered close to the Egyptian side of Aqaba, which led Ron to conclude that the chariot would have been at the back of the marching army. The chariots of priests were not as sturdy as the ones the infantrymen used in battle.

As stated before the Wyatts found several six-spoked wheels and an eight-spoked wheel. The six-spoked wheel (next photo) from Tutankhamun's (King Tut) tomb is in the Cairo Museum. It shows a wheel that had not deteriorated in the Red Sea. The six-spoked wheel in King Tut's tomb and other artifacts from 3,465 years ago are a silent testimony to the *fact* that the Red Sea crossing was a real event—a God-orchestrated, miraculous event—in which more than two million Hebrew people were saved from mistreatment at the hands of the Egyptians. One of the wheels that Ron Wyatt found had a hub with eight spokes remaining. He took this to Nassif Mohammed Hassan, director of antiquities in Cairo. Hassan examined the artifact and declared it to be from the eighteenth Dynasty of ancient Egypt.

Six-Spoked Wheel in King Tut's Tomb

covenantkeepers.co.uk

I had never done a lot of thinking about the devastation caused in Egypt when the Israelites left. For one thing, they had lost all their Hebrew servants. They were preparing royal funerals. And the Egyptian people were dealing with deaths in their own families, the death of a child—or possibly an adult— and they were getting rid of the carcasses of their firstborn livestock. On top of all that, the king, the priesthood, and the entire Egyptian army had disappeared. The discovery of the wheels and other artifacts are valuable physical evidence for the Red Sea crossing. The data gained from the chariot wheels placed the Exodus at the time of the Eighteenth Dynasty. Amazingly, this is the most well-documented group of kings in all of ancient Egypt.

For ten years, Ron Wyatt faithfully pursued his dreams of uncovering and discovering more and more evidence of God's hand at work on planet earth. Egyptian chariots were also discovered on the Saudi side of the Gulf of Aqaba. This means that the Egyptian army (Josephus estimated 250,000 men) was stretched out over the entire eight (some quote nine and a half miles) while the Red Sea was being restrained by God before it came crashing down.

A professor of archaeology at the University of North Carolina Chapel Hill, Jodi Magness, discovered an interesting confirmation of the Red Sea crossing on a hill above the Sea of Galilee in northern Israel. A *National Geographic* article stated that a confirmation of the Red Sea crossing is depicted in the mosaics. The Roman-era synagogue at the site of Huqoq, Israel, is the site of amazing fifth-century mosaics that depict the parting of the Red Sea. Magness said, "You can see the pharaoh's soldiers with their chariots and horses drowning and being eaten by large fish." Another scene shows several sinuous fish, a horse floating upside down, and soldiers with shields and spears being swept off their feet as the waters of the Red Sea crash in on them. Another of the mosaics that Dr. Magness exposed depicted two of every living thing that marched into Noah's ark before the Great Flood (Genesis 6–9).

In the *National Geographic* article, Dr. Jodi Magness confirmed the Exodus, which is also called the Red Sea crossing. The mosaics that her project unearthed depict:

- Egyptian soldiers with their chariots and horses drowning,
- Egyptian soldiers being eaten by large fish,
- Egyptian soldiers under water bearing shields and spears,
- Egyptian soldiers being swept off their feet by the Red Sea waters, and
- A horse floating upside down.

These facts add a new dimension of reality and confirm a Red Sea crossing (Gulf of Aqaba) as the Holy Scriptures so vividly portray. And there was a nation, a group of people who had descended from Abraham and Sarah. They had been invited by a pharaoh in the days of Joseph to live in a choice place called Goshen (Land of Ramses) in the Nile River Delta. The number of them was seventy. Over the course of 430 years, the Lord blessed them and increased their number to "about 600,000 on foot that were men, beside children" (Exodus 12:37). Other versions of the Bible add women as well. An earlier chart explained how this number was close to two million people.

If there are people still doubting, who think that there was not enough space for two million Hebrews plus two hundred fifty thousand Egyptians on one beach called Nuweiba, the diagram below should help shed new light. These calculations reveal that only 2.6% of the Nuweiba Beach was covered by people. This left ample space for the chariots of the Egyptians and the livestock of the Israelites. A chariot would take up more space than a person and of course the livestock would have taken up even more space than a chariot. To summarize there would definitely have been ample space on the Nuweiba Beach for all the Israelites plus their livestock, all the Egyptians, and their chariots.

Nuweiba Beach

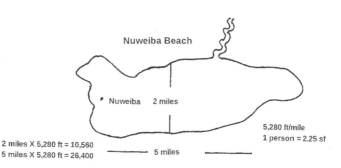

Nuweiba Beach

Nuweiba   2 miles

5,280 ft/mile
1 person = 2.25 sf

2 miles X 5,280 ft = 10,560
5 miles X 5,280 ft = 26,400   5 miles

10,560 X 26,400 = 278,784,000 sf a 5 X 2 rectangle
278,784,000 X .70 = 195,148,800
estimate due to the rounded corners of the island
2.25 sf/person; 2,000,000 persons
2.25 X 2,000,000 = 4,500,000 sf for the Hebrews
2.25 X   250,000 = + 562,500 sf for the Egyptians
5,062,500
195,148,800 - 5,062,500 = 190,086,300 sf remaining

The Middle East is a big place, and finding the exact Biblical spots could be difficult. Mr. Wyatt and his sons were looking for evidence that the Egyptians had actually drowned in the Gulf of Aqaba as the waters rolled back. Moses and two million Israelites had passed through the eight to nine-mile land bridge on dry ground: "a way in the sea, and a path in the mighty waters" (Isaiah 43:16).

Many degreed archaeologists have searched for years without finding the biblical sites. This lack of success in finding the true sites is probably due to a lot of confusion from the fourth century. Mt. Sinai has been noted in the wrong place on many maps. It has been placed on the Sinai Peninsula instead of Midian in Saudi Arabia. In order to find these biblical places, Ron Wyatt relied heavily on the scriptures. He also believed that the Lord had miraculously showed him many times where to look.

Several examples are recorded in the work of Ron Wyatt when the Lord showed him where to look. In the search for Noah's ark, for instance, he and his sons prayed a short prayer that the Lord would guide them before they got into a taxi headed in the direction of where the ark remains might be located. The taxi stalled three times, and they placed a pile of rocks beside the road where the taxi stalled each time. (This doesn't sound very scientific or cool, but it is how God showed the Wyatts one of the locations of His Treasures.) These three piles of rock became the points that led them to discover what is now The Noah's Ark National Park in Turkey; it is also sometimes referred to as the Durupinar Site.

Another example occurred when they became curious about strange shapes in the sand as they traveled the highways in Israel. This led them to find another of God's Treasures: the remains of Sodom and Gomorrah. On a third occasion, Ron got sunburned feet from diving into the Red Sea (Gulf of Aqaba). The sunburned feet temporarily prevented further Aqaba exploration. They decided to take a break and explore Jerusalem. As they walked around, Ron suddenly pointed to a garbage pile, that he had not even considered looking at as the location for the Ark of the Covenant. Months of digging in the Garden Tomb led to no results. He went back to work as an anesthetist in a hospital in Tennessee to earn more money for doing more excavating later.

Sometime later, on a return trip to the Middle East, while Ron was forming a team and seeking permission to search for the Ark of the Covenant, God continued to lead Ron on his path of discovery. Many visits to the Israeli Antiquities Authority for permits to excavate proved fruitless. Therefore, the team decided to take a day off and go swimming at Ashkelon on the Mediterranean Sea. As they swam, Ron's foot hit an object. The object turned out to be a Philistine burial pot that archaeologists working with the Israeli Antiquities Authority had searched for so many years. The Antiquities Authority was so thrilled with the find that permits to dig for the Ark of the Covenant were granted immediately. These and many other stories abound regarding the ways that the Lord guided Ron Wyatt to find His Treasures.

Now that it is clearly documented by the evidence Ron Wyatt first found in 1978, it is amazing that up-to-date authorities like Wikipedia and others still are blind and include statements to the effect that Moses and the crossing of the Red Sea is a myth. Once a couple of months ago when I brought up Wikipedia on my computer, the true biblical story was given as it occurred in the Bible. Then the Wikipedia article continued and stated,

Ron Wyatt has produced photos showing what *appears* to be chariot wheels at the bottom of the Red Sea and submitted a wheel hub to Nassid Mohammed Hassan, Director of Antiquities in Cairo.

And a *New York Times* article from April 3, 2007 discusses the Exodus, Passover, the Israelites' biblical flight from Egypt, and the forty years of wandering the desert in search of the Promised land. Michael Slackman quoted Zahi Hawass, an

Egyptian archaeologist and formerly Egypt's Minister of State for Antiquities Affairs:

No archaeological *scholarly* verified evidence has been found that confirms that the crossing of the Red Sea ever took place. Really, it's a myth. Sometimes as archaeologists, we have to say that never happened because there is no *historical evidence.*

The key words here are: *appears, scholarly,* and *historical.* If Ron Wyatt had not been an amateur archaeologist, but was one of the elite archaeologists with letters after their names, like PhD, do you think that a discovery of this magnitude way back in 1978 would not have been applauded by the scientific community as the find of the century? As a former science teacher in the public schools for forty-three years, I struggled with articles like this and the unbelief that it portrays.

After hours of contemplation, I think I have the answer. A story from the Holy Bible brings this situation into clear focus. If the trained, real archaeologists don't read the Bible and don't follow the clues written there then how could they expect to find these elusive Biblical artifacts. Ron Wyatt followed the clues and found the land bridge across the Gulf of Aqaba. The results are that some scientists, being closed-minded to the facts right in front of their faces would not even accept and believe—even if Jesus made a personal appearance and told them.

Luke illustrates this more clearly in the story of the rich man and Lazarus:

There was a certain rich man, which was clothed in purple and fine linen, and fared sumptuously every day: And there was a certain beggar named Lazarus, which was laid at his gate, full of sores, And desiring to be fed with the crumbs which fell from the rich man's table: moreover the dogs came and licked his sores. And it came to pass, that the beggar died, and was carried by the angels into Abraham's bosom: the rich man also died, and was buried; And in hell he lifts up his eyes, being in torments, and seeth Abraham afar off, and Lazarus in his bosom. And he cried and said, Father Abraham, have mercy on me, and send Lazarus, that he may dip the tip of his finger in water, and cool my tongue; for I am tormented in this flame. But Abraham said, Son, remember that thou in thy lifetime received thy good things, and likewise Lazarus evil things: but now he is comforted, and thou art tormented. And beside all this, between us and you there is a great gulf fixed: so that they which would pass from hence to you cannot; neither can they pass to us, that would come from thence. Then he said, I pray thee therefore, father, that thou wouldest send him to my father's house: For I have five brothers; that he may testify unto them, lest they also come into this place of torment. Abraham saith unto him, They have Moses and the prophets; let them hear them. And he said, Nay, father Abraham: but if one went unto them from the dead, they will repent. And he said unto him, If they hear not Moses and the prophets, neither will they be persuaded, though one rose from the dead." (Luke 16:19–31)

Why do the vast majority of scholars reject this Red Sea discovery? *True Discoveries* (19) addresses this very topic:

Michael Lemonick would tell us that "most scholars suspect that Abraham, Isaac and Jacob never existed; many doubt the tales of slavery in Egypt and the Exodus" (*Time*, December 18, 1995.)

A quote from *True Discoveries* (18) should ease the mind of anyone who might be concerned regarding the safety of these valuable artifacts.

One shudders to think what might be happening to the irreplaceable evidence of the destruction of Pharaoh's hosts in the Red Sea once Ron Wyatt and others revealed the true site. This information would undoubtedly draw hordes of scavengers and treasure seekers who would be well aware of the value of ancient artifacts. How could these historic objects survive? The remains, fortunately, are largely covered with coral, which has preserved them and helped disguise their presence. Fortunately, most of the remains are on the Saudi Arabian side of the sea, which is out of bounds to tourists and divers. Any divers at the Egyptian side must now report to a local police officer—and no artifacts are allowed out of Egypt.

Pharaoh's Drowned Army

THE RED SEA

Pharaoh's Drowned Army

Confirmation of the actual Exodus route has come from divers finding coral-encrusted bones and chariot remains in the Gulf of Aqaba

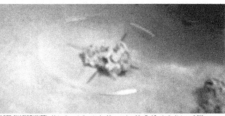

GILDED CHARIOT WHEEL - Mute witness to the miracle of the crossing of the Red Sea by the Hebrews 3,500 years ago

Report from the Gulf of Aqaba.
The discovery of THE EXODUS ROUTE

ONE of the most dramatic records of Divine intervention in history is the account of the Hebrews' exodus from Egypt.

The subsequent drowning of the entire Egyptian army in the Red Sea was not an insignificant event, and confirmation of this event is compelling evidence that the Biblical narrative is truly authentic.

Over the years, many divers have searched the Gulf of Suez in vain for artefacts to verify the Biblical account. But carefully following the Biblical and historical records of the Exodus brings you to Nuweiba, a large beach in the Gulf of Aqaba, as Ron Wyatt discovered in 1978.

Repeated dives in depths ranging from 60 to 200 feet deep (18m to 60m), over a stretch of almost 2.5 km, has shown that the chariot parts are scattered across the sea bed.

Artefacts found include wheels,

chariot bodies as well as human and horse bones. Divers have located wreckage on the Saudi coastline opposite Nuweiba as well.

Since 1987, Ron Wyatt found three 4-spoked gilded chariot wheels. Coral does not grow on gold, hence the shape has remained very distinct, although the wood inside the gold veneer has disintegrated making them too fragile to move.

The hope for future expeditions is to explore the deeper waters with remote cameras or mini-subs.

4-Spoked Wheel, (above) filmed by Ron Wyatt on the seabed off Nuweiba, is identical to the 4-spoke wheel used in ancient Egypt.
The illustration from Egyptian tomb paintings (below), shows how these were constructed.

Mineralised Bone - One of several recovered from the crossing site (above right) next to a modern equivalent (above left). The Dept. of Ontcology at Stockholm University found it to be a human femur, from the right leg of a 165-170cm tall man. radiocarbon dating methods are not applicable as it is essentially 'fossilized' i.e. replaced by minerals and coral, although this specimen is obviously from antiquity.

Coral-encrusted chariot wheel filmed off the Saudi coastline, matches chariot wheels found in Tutankhamen's tomb.

Chariot from Tutankhamen's tomb on display in the Cairo Museum

6-Spoke Wheel

Illustration from "The Ancient Egyptians" by Sir J. Gardiner Wilkinson

How deep is the water?

THE Gulf of Aqaba is very deep. In places over a mile (1,600m) deep.

Even with the sea dried up, walking across would be difficult due to the steep grade down the sides. But there is one spot where if the water were removed, it would be an easy descent for people and animals. This is the line between Nuweiba and the opposite shore in Saudi Arabia.

Depth sounding expeditions have revealed a smooth, gentle slope descending from Nuweiba out into the Gulf. This shows up almost like a pathway on depth-recording equipment, confirming it's Biblical description *"...a way in the sea, and a path in the mighty waters." (Isaiah 43:16)*

The Bible writers frequently refer to the miracle of the Red Sea crossing, for it was an event which finds no equal in history. The Hebrew prophets describe the sea at the crossing site as *"...the waters of the great deep ...the depths of the sea..." (Isaiah 51:10)*

Having found the exact spot which the Bible writers were referring to, what is the water depth? The distance between Nuweiba and where artifacts have been found on Saudi coast is about 18km (11 miles). Along this line the deepest point is still 800m (½ mile) deep!

No wonder that the Inspired writers of the Bible described it as the mighty waters. And no wonder that none in that mighty army survived when the water collapsed in upon them.

NUWEIBA BEACH - The beach where the crossing began

Solomon's memorial pillars

WHEN Ron Wyatt first visited Nuweiba in 1978, he found a Phoenician style column lying in the water.

Unfortunately the inscription had been eroded away, hence its column's importance was not understood until 1984, when a second Phoenician column was found on the Saudi coastline opposite -- identical, except on this one the inscription was still intact.

In Phoenician letters (Archaic Hebrew), it contained the words: *Mizraim* (Egypt), *Solomon*, *Edom*, *death*, *Pharaoh*, *Moses*; and *Yahweh*, indicating that King Solomon had set up these columns as a memorial to the miracle of the crossing of the sea.

Saudi Arabia does not admit tourists, and perhaps fearing unauthorized visitors, the Saudi Authorities subsequently removed this column, and replaced it with a flag marker where it once stood.

BIBLICAL EVIDENCE	
THE EXODUS ROUTE	
A few examples of how this discovery matches the clues found in the Biblical record	
BIBLE CLUES	**ACTUAL FINDINGS**
Exodus 13:18 - Israel had led Egypt before crossing the Red Sea	They had departed from Egypt - Had the crossing been through the Gulf of Suez Canal, they would have still been in Egypt when they began crossing
Exodus 13:18 - They crossed the 'wilderness of the Red sea'	They crossed the desert between the two arms of the Red sea - called today the Sinai Peninsula, its ancient name was the "Wilderness of the Red sea"
Exodus 14:3 - They would appear to be 'entangled' and 'shut in'	The Exodus route led through a long canyon - called "Wadi Watir", it is the only route to Nuweiba from the wilderness, and fits this description perfectly
Exodus 3:1,12 - Moses led the people to a mountain in Midian	Midian is in north eastern Saudi Arabia - hence Moses led the Israelites to a mountain in Arabia, not on the Sinai peninsula as is commonly believed today
Much more evidence is available!	See details on page 8

MEDITERRANEAN SEA

THE EXODUS ROUTE - With the correct crossing site in the Gulf of Aqaba

CHAPTER 5
Mt. Sinai

Final Temporary Destination, Mt. Sinai

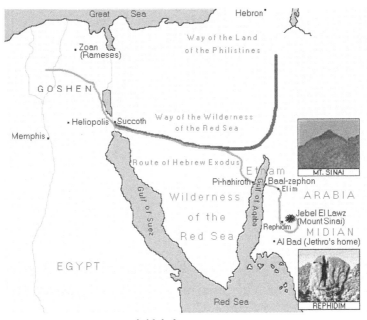

biblebelievers.org.au

THE PREVIOUS MAP (*Bible Believers*, 1) clearly shows the route of the Exodus from Goshen through Succoth. The trip to Etham was a sidetrack initiated by God to confuse the pharaoh. Next, the two million Israelites wound their way through the

Wadi Watir to the Gulf of Aqaba. As you know, the Israelites all passed through Aqaba on the dry land of the eight-to-nine-and-a-half-mile land bridge to their destination in Saudi Arabia. And the evidence of the demise of the Egyptian army is preserved by coral on the floor of the Gulf of Aqaba.

Israeli Encampment Area

arkdiscovery.com

This image of the Israeli Encampment Area shows the land at the base of Mt. Sinai in Saudi Arabia where the two million people lived for forty years. Not only had God supplied a huge beach that had enough room for all the Hebrews, their livestock, the Egyptians, their chariots and horses but on the other side of the Red Sea He provided a sufficiently large area for them to live. This area was bounded and protected by the surrounding mountains. When God created this area it was not a problem for Him to create the huge NUweiba Beach on the Egyptina side and now a huge encampment area on the Saudi side. According to Ark Discovery there are thousands of acres for camping at the base of this mountain.

Mt. Sinai (Jebel al-Lawz)

biblebelievers.org.au

It can clearly be seen in this photograph that there is a straight line across the peak where the fire ended. This is not a shadow made by a cloud hiding the sun. The lighter rock (see photo) is igneous, and the darker rock above the line is former igneous rock that has been metamorphosed (cooked so to speak). The natural process of turning igneous rock (granite) to metamorphic rock (basalt) occurs from volcanic processes which produce extreme heat. I have watched YouTube videos in which the climbers who go to the peak of Mt. Sinai use a geology hammer to crack the black rock. When they do, the rock under the surface is not dark—it is light—which shows that the fire that descended by God (Exodus 19:18) was only on the surface and did not penetrate the entire rock.

Mt. Sinai was covered with smoke, because the Lord descended on it in fire. The smoke billowed up from it like smoke from a furnace, and the whole mountain trembled violently. (Exodus 19:18)

According to an article from *Covenant Keepers*, Dr. Glen Fritz believed the rock composing Mt. Sinai was granite; however, after God's fire, the black rock on the summit became basalt, which is normally formed in nature from the heat of volcanoes.

Rock Samples from Mt. Sinai

covenantkeepers.co.uk

The preceding map from *Bible Believers* (1) seems to wrap up the entire story of the crossing of the Red Sea (Gulf of Aqaba). It shows us that the land of Midian is located in Saudi Arabia and not the Sinai Peninsula.

However, they did meet the Wadi Alfa, cutting in a north-south direction, after they traveled eastward. Veering left and traveling the Wadi Alfa between mountains, they arrived in an open plain. Next, they turned east into the foothills of the western side of Jebel al-Lawz (also called Mt. Sinai, Horeb, and Moses's Mountain). They had set out from the Desert of Sin(ai) and arrived at a place called Rephidim. Then the people became very angry with Moses because of a lack of water. If God had just saved them from the angry Egyptians, wouldn't they have considered praying rather than complaining to poor Moses?

Moses grew quite tired of the complaints:

And all the congregation of the children of Israel journeyed from the Wilderness of Sin, after their journeys, according to the commandment of the Lord, and pitched in Rephidim: and there was no water for the people to drink. Wherefore the people did chide with Moses, and said, Give us water that we may drink. And Moses said unto them, Why chide ye with me? Wherefore do ye tempt the Lord? And the people thirsted there for water; and the people murmured against Moses, and said, Wherefore is this that thou hast brought us up out of Egypt, to kill us and our children and our cattle with thirst? And Moses cried unto the Lord, saying, What shall I do unto this people? They be almost ready to stone me. And the Lord said unto Moses, Go on before the people, and take with thee of the elders of Israel; and thy rod, wherewith thou smotest the river, take in thine hand, and go. Behold, I will stand before thee there upon the rock in Horeb; and thou shalt smite the rock, and there shall come water out of it, that the people may drink. And Moses did so in the sight of the elders of Israel. And he called the name of the place Massah, and Meribah, because of the chiding of the children of Israel, and because they tempted the Lord, saying, Is the Lord among us, or not? (Exodus 17:1–7)

Split Rock at Mt. Horeb

covenantkeepers.co.uk

God caused water to gush out of the "rock at Horeb." (*True Discoveries, 39*)

The close-up photograph of the split rock at Mount Horeb clearly shows a lot of water erosion on the stones downstream from the rock. This is where God told Moses to strike the rock (Exodus 17:5–7). A second time and in a different place (Numbers 20:11) when God asked Moses to speak to the rock in order to get water for the Israelites, he disobeyed God. In his anger he not only struck the rock once but he struck it twice. God was not pleased, and because of Moses' disobedience, he and his brother Aaron were banned from entering Canaan, the Promised Land.

In 1984 Ron Wyatt and his sons discovered Mt. Sinai hours before they were falsely arrested and sent to jail. (story covered in detail in the next chapter). Among the items that they discovered were Egyptian-style drawings of calves (*Discovery News*). Since these drawings were found nowhere else in Saudi Arabia, this further confirmed the location had been inhabited by people from Egypt (i.e. the Israelites).

When Mr. Wyatt saw broken pieces of columns strewn about, he remembered reading Exodus 24:4: And Moses wrote all the words of the Lord, and rose up early in the morning, and built an altar under the hill, and twelve pillars, according to the twelve tribes of Israel.

Marble Pillars

covenantkeepers.co.uk

Pillar Measurements

covenantkeepers.co.uk

Ron Wyatt also discovered tiny flecks of gold reflected in the water of a depression in the worn rock. Could this have been the remains after so many years of the gold powder left from Moses grinding the idol, the golden calf, and making the people drink it (Exodus 32:20)? Ron also discovered what appeared to be an elaborate water supply system. A lot of water would have been needed by the more than two million people plus their animals since they lived there for a year.

Tree Between Two Rock

true discoveries.org

When Ron saw the mountain above the cave, he observed a lone tree growing between two huge boulders, which was unusual because the area has a large amount of granite. It does not seem possible that a tree of that size could have managed to grow in such harsh terrain. The cave being referred to is Elijah's Cave.

And he (Elijah) came thither unto a cave, and lodged there; and, behold, the word of the Lord came to him, and he said unto him, What doest thou here, Elijah? And he said, I have been very zealous for the Lord God of hosts: for the children of Israel have forsaken thy covenant, thrown down thine altars, and slain thy prophets with the sword; and I, even I only, am left; and they seek my life, to take it away. And he said, Go forth, and stand upon the mount before the Lord (1 King 19:9-11)

Aaron Sen at the Fence

covenantkeepers.co.uk

At some point after Ron Wyatt discovered Mt. Sinai in 1984 the Saudi government erected a chain-link fence around this area. The photo of Aaron Sen was taken in May 2003 showing the fence. However, during this trip which included Professor Lennart Moller, Andrew Jones, and Mahoney Media the group was invited past the guard tower. As can be seen from the sign this was very unusual. The group was able to climb up the blackened peak of Mt. Sinai. The Saudi government has not been open to allowing people to enter the area. In English on the sign, the government calls it an archaeological area.

Mt. Sinai Located in Arabia

SAUDI ARABIA

Mt Sinai located in Arabia

MOUNT SINAI - the mountain from which God spoke the 10 commandments in smoke and fire, is blackened and scorched

The mountain peak scorched by Supernatural heat

Report from northwest Saudi Arabia
The discovery of MOUNT SINAI

Cartographers have traditionally placed Mt Sinai in what is today referred to as the Sinai Peninsular.

Every year pilgrims flock to the traditional mountain. But knowing the location of the Red Sea crossing site at the Gulf of Aqaba, it becomes obvious that the real Mt. Sinai must be in Saudi Arabia. The Bible itself bears witness to this fact, *"...Mount Sinai in Arabia"* (Galatians 4.25).

The mountain now believed to be the Biblical Mount Sinai is known on modern maps as Jebel el Lawz. This mountain encloses an area large enough to accommodate millions of people and their flocks and herds.

The mountain's peak has been blackened. Exodus 19:18 records *"And mount Sinai was altogether on a smoke, because the LORD descended upon it in fire, and the smoke thereof ascended as the smoke of a furnace."*

Mt Sinai - a protected archeological site

The site shows all the evidence of being an encampment for millions of people. The are ancient tent sites, evidence of a vast water supply, and even the altar upon which the Golden Calf was erected.

After Ron Wyatt drew attention to this site in 1984, the Saudi Authorities erected a wire mesh fence around the base, and declared the area as an archeological site, off limits to unauthorized personnel.

Water from the rock

The Rock in Horeb - The close-up reveals the significant water erosion

THE evidence of another Biblical miracle is still standing today!

At the Lord's command, Moses smote what the Bible refers to as "the rock" in Horeb. Fresh water gushed forth, supplying the Hebrews, and their flocks for the two years they encamped there.

Man-made channels run out from the rock into the plain, where the Hebrews would have been encamped, precisely what one would expect to find.

Altar of the Golden Calf

Protected - Now fenced off by the Authorities

AT the base of Jabel el Lawz is a large altar, with Egyptian Apis bulls, or calves, inscribed onto it.

When Ron Wyatt showed this altar to an archaeologist from Rejhard University, he immediately recognised the significance of it. There is no other site like it in Saudi Arabia.

The story of the Golden Calf, in chapter 32 of Exodus, is well known, and now at last the actual altar has been found. However until the Saudi Authorities allow access to foreigners, viewing the site is extremely difficult. Yet despite this, some have successfully done so.

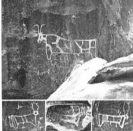

Apis Bulls Egyptian cult worship in Saudi Arabia, as in Exodus 32

Ron Wyatt: The Scientific approach

Ronald Wyatt - Recognised for his significant work on the Noah's Ark site

The man behind these discoveries
A profile of Ronald B. Wyatt by Bill Fry

THE work which Ron was led to accomplish, confirming the validity of the Word of God, is touching an ever growing number of lives.

Ron Wyatt was not a professional archeologist. He was an anaesthetist by profession. He began his personal research into ancient history, the sciences and the Bible as a young man, motivated by his own curiosity.

In 1977 Ron began field work in Turkey. In 1978 he began work in Egypt, and in 1979, Israel. At first his "team" consisted of himself and his two teenaged sons, and later, other interested individuals offered their assistance. At the time of his death in August of 1999, Ron had made over 120 trips to the Middle East.

Ron funded most of his work himself. Over the years, several individuals who believed in his work also provided some financial assistance. His work was based on his profound belief in the total accuracy of the Biblical account, and on this basis, his general policy was to share these evidences with "those who ask".

Because Ron Wyatt's "Discoveries" testify to the veracity of the Biblical narrative, they are quite controversial in both the scientific and scholarly communities. As a result, Ron never looked to scientists or scholars to "confirm" them. He employed scientific testing, then presented the evidence from those tests and the testimony of experts as to the results. He then presented the body of evidence, biblical, historical, archaeological and scientific, in the belief that each individual was capable of making their own decision.

Ronald Wyatt passed away on the 4th of August, 1999. He is greatly missed by those knew and worked with him. Many of these individuals are now carrying on the work he began.

Noah's Ark Press Conference with Governor Sevket Ekinci of the Agri district, Eastern Turkey

With Tom Jarrell during the filming of ABC's "20/20" report on Noah's Ark

On CNN - Showing the laminated wood recovered from Noah's Ark

With Col. James Irwin - who also searched for Noah's Ark

With Dr. Ali Hassan head of the Egyptian Antiquities

CHAPTER 6
Incarceration

RON WYATT AND his sons discovered the real Mt. Sinai in 1984. After so much praying and seeing the items mentioned in the Bible, actually being in Saudi Arabia made them feel totally elated. Even before Mr. Wyatt set foot on Middle Eastern soil, his mind was fully engaged in the area. According to *Anchor Stone* (1–5), he saw a mountain range as he studied some flight maps of the area while he was waiting for a visa to enter Saudi Arabia. The mountain range was in northwestern Saudi Arabia with a high peak called Jebel al-Lawz. This appeared to him to be the correct mountain based on what he had read in the Bible regarding Mt. Sinai.

The Lord our God spoke unto us in Horeb, saying, "Ye have dwelt long enough in this mount" (Deuteronomy 1:6). It had canyons, called wadis, that were wide and spacious enough for the Israelites and their livestock. The area was also protected by all the surrounding mountains and separated from the mountains paralleling the Red Sea by a desert that he thought might be the Desert of Sinai. As Ron studied the area of Jebel al-Lawz, he realized that he had to see the mountain for himself in order to confirm that it was the true Mt. Sinai.

Since a visa was required in order to enter Saudi Arabia,

Mr. Wyatt spent four and a half years applying for visas for he and his sons. Finally he had to face the fact that Saudi Arabia would not be honoring his requests for visas. Ron, not being a lawless person, had researched the penalty for being caught without a visa. While it would be inconvenient, the penalty was mild and would only involve being escorted to the border and kicked out. The worst-case scenario would be a detention of twenty-one days.

But to be on the safe side, before leaving the United States, he had confided in two "trusted" friends: Colonel Jim Irwin, the astronaut, and another person. Since I have never seen this man's name in a public document by Ron Wyatt, I will not place his name here. Ron told his two friends that he planned to go into Saudi Arabia without visas to confirm that the real Mt. Sinai was located in Saudi Arabia—and not on the Sinai Peninsula as all the Bible maps seem to indicate. Finally, after more than four years of not receiving visas from Saudi Arabia, he obtained them from Jordan.

Upon entering Jordan on January 24, 1984, Ron Wyatt, his sons, Daniel, sixteen, and Ronald Jr., eighteen, parked their rental car and walked into Saudi Arabia illegally since no visa from Saudi Arabia had been forthcoming for four and a half years. They hitchhiked and hired taxis in order to get to Jebel al-Lawz.

The mountain was confirmed due to the blackened top from the time when God had sent fire down onto it: "Mt. Sinai was covered with smoke, because the Lord descended on it in fire. The smoke billowed up from it like smoke from a furnace, and the whole mountain trembled violently" (Exodus 19:18). They also saw white pillars on the ground.

The following photo shows the actor, Charlton Heston (as Moses) holding the stone containing the law, with Mt.

Sinai in the background. This award winning movie, The Ten Commandments dates back to 1956. The director was Cecil B. DeMille who had previously directed a movie with the same topic in 1923.

The Real Mt. Sinai in Saudi Arabia

arkdiscovery.com

Egyptian Style Drawings of Calf

arkdiscovery.com

Being here was such a 'dream come true' and their visit had been so successful; they were totally unprepared for the next series of events that would soon take place. As was mentioned earlier Ron and his sons found white pillars with broken pieces strewn on the ground. There were tiny flecks of gold found in the water that had collected in a worn rock. Ron even saw on the mountain above the cave (of Ezekiel) a lone tree growing between two boulders. It did not seem possible that a tree of that size could have managed to grow in such harsh terrain where there appeared to be no soil just particles of granite. They also found an altar with Egyptian-style drawings of calves.

Intending to exit the country and return to their rental car, which was parked in Jordan, they were arrested by Saudi officials as Israeli spies and taken to a jail near the border in Haig. It was discovered later that the "trusted friend" had been the source of the accusation. They were not accused of being just any old spies; Israeli spies were the archenemies of the Saudis.

Arriving at the jail, there was little time to comprehend the gravity of their situation because there was a full-blown plague going on. Many prisoners had died already, and those who had not died were gravely ill. Ron, having been educated as an anesthetist, quickly assessed the situation. He convinced the Saudis that he was a sleep doctor who could help the prisoners with medicine. This resulted in him being able to write prescriptions for antibiotics, which the Haig pharmacy honored. The antibiotics taken with aspirin, immediately helped the patients' discomfort.

Ron realized that the mosquitoes, which swarmed everywhere, were the real source of the epidemic. Next, he requested and was given huge amounts of olive oil to pour into the toilets and standing water to kill the mosquito larvae. Easing the plague gave the Wyatts some favor with the authorities.

Daily, Ron and his sons were interrogated separately by an interrogation team. The three men never changed their story because they believed that Jebel al-Lawz was the real mountain of Moses, Mt. Sinai. There was some hope for a short time when a Saudi official, Abu Collet, sent men to the mountain in search of evidence. They found no evidence, and their report for the king was negative. After the negative report, their hopes of finding favor with the Saudis were dashed. But perhaps on the other hand their unchanging ideas regarding the location of Mt. Sinai would eventually be believed by some Saudis.

This was a typical scenario in the search for God's Treasures. All of the many attempts by individuals, groups, and even a Russian led expedition to Mt. Ararat in 1916-1918 to find Noah's Ark failed. Many times the documentation was lost, and in some cases lives were also lost in these endeavors. As you will learn later the Wyatts also lost all their film and thus their documentation. I believe that God is very much in control of the timing of the exposition of His treasures: Noah's Ark, the Tower of Babel, Sodom and Gomorrah, the Ark of the Covenant, the Red Sea crossing, and Mt. Sinai.

Mr. Wyatt was in for a big surprise when he was invited to go on a helicopter ride. The destination was a beach on the Saudi side of the Gulf of Aqaba to look at the huge column that had been placed there by King Solomon. It was placed there to mark the place where the Israelites had walked onto Saudi soil after crossing the Red Sea.

Once they landed, Nuweiba Beach in Egypt was clearly visible across the eight miles (some references say nine and a half miles). Approximately two million Israelites had walked on dry land to freedom in Saudi Arabia. The Phoenician-style column was made of granite and was standing upright.

Kevin Fisher at Egyptian Column

Arkdiscovery.com

The inscriptions on the Saudi column were written in ancient Hebrew. The translation read: "Mizraim (Egypt), Solomon, Edom, Death, Pharaoh, Moses Yahweh." The pillar has since been removed and replaced by a marker. Ron had found the matching column on the Egyptian side in 1978, but it had no legible writing. The columns were erected by King Solomon four hundred years after the crossing to mark the location. The king's seaport was at Eilat, on the northern tip of the Gulf of Aqaba. (Isaiah 19:19) Ron Wyatt (7) gives God the credit for using the column to save their lives.

After more than two months in jail, the youngest son was beginning to be unable to cope. He informed his dad that he could not tolerate the situation any longer. He was going to make a run for it. His dad realized that the son would be shot and told him to wait until Thursday, the Muslim holy day. Everyone would be focused on the holy day, and they would have a better chance of getting free.

As it turned out Ali, a guard friendly to them was on duty that day. Ron told his son that if they made a run for it on Ali's watch, he would be shot. They decided to wait for the following

Thursday. Maybe Ali was on duty to save them from escaping at all.

On the day before the planned escape, the man in charge said they had been cleared and would be turned over to the Jordanian government; however, all of their film, which would verify the location of Mt. Sinai, was confiscated. They were detained in Jordan for another three days—and then they were finally released to go home.

Ron and his sons were incarcerated for seventy-five days. This shows the type of sacrifice and hard work that he exerted from 1978, when he first dove into the Gulf of Aqaba. He found the remains of the Egyptian army there and continued his explorations of other sites until his death due to cancer in August 1999. When they were released after the seventy-five-day ordeal, the Saudi embassy told Ron the name of the man whom Ron had confided in about his trip to Saudi Arabia. This individual had lied when he said that Ron and his sons were Israeli spies. The Saudis were very angry and wanted to help Ron prosecute the man who had almost perpetrated a very ugly international event. Ron declined their offer, and in so doing, he exhibited the same kind of godly behavior that was a foundational part of the fabric of his life.

In the discoveries that Ron Wyatt so faithfully pursued not only was he falsely accused of being a spy but thieves have tried more than once to steal Ron Wyatt's hard work. However, God will only allow them to go so far. Why have all the archaeologists with letters after their names tried for years to discover these treasures, only to fail again and again? God guided Moses and the Israelites through the wilderness, and then He guided Ron Wyatt, an amateur archaeologist in the twentieth century, to find them all. It is not difficult to confirm; a click of the mouse is all it takes to find what I have exposed in this book. The entire account of the incarceration in Saudi Arabia was taken from ronwyatt.com.

CBS Morning News

CBS News Archives

Ron and his sons were featured on the CBS nationally televised Morning News on Tuesday, April 17, 1984. Ron explained the circumstances and why he had "snuck" into Saudi Arabia without visas. The entire ordeal of the seventy-five day incarceration in a Saudi Arabian jail had now made the national news in the United States. Amazingly, Ron Wyatt's desire to set the record straight had been realized. Now the world would know that Mt. Sinai had been incorrectly placed on maps on the Sinai Peninsula since the fourth century. However, as history would show it would be thirty-five years and six months until Saudi Arabia would open its gates to tourism and visits to the *'REAL' Mt. Sinai*. Justice was served when one year later *Ron* was exonerated by being legally invited to enter Saudi Arabia by Samran Al Motairy.

In conclusion, the Bible—together with the physical evidence provided in large part by Ron Wyatt—seems to prove beyond any doubt that Moses did indeed lead the Israelites through the dry seafloor of the Red Sea (Gulf of Aqaba) as is stated in the Bible (Exodus 3–17). Furthermore, it has been shown that Mt. Sinai (Jebel al-Lawz), is located in Midian, which is in Saudi Arabia. The following image seems to wrap up the entire story by providing a visual image of the Red Sea (Gulf of Aqaba) with Mt. Sinai in the correct place in Saudi Arabia.

Map of the Red Sea Crossing

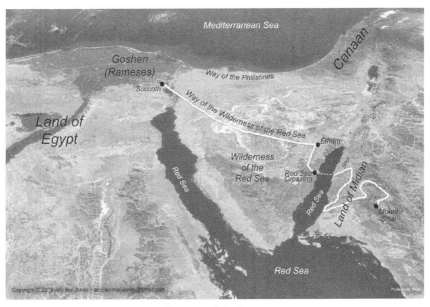

discoveredsinai.com

CBN Newsbreak
Faithwire October 17, 2019

Saudi Arabia to Allow Access to Ancient Biblical Sites, Including the "Real" Mount Sinai

After being closed to tourism for the past few decades, Saudi Arabia is not only allowing tourists to visit but opening their doors for those who want to see the biblical sites the country has to offer. The move to allow tourism comes following the second meeting of evangelical leaders from America, with Saudi Crown Prince Mohammed bin Salman.3

—CBN News

A miraculous series of events occurred in October 2019: the Saudi government opened up its country to tourism. Due to the high level of interest in the Exodus and Moses on Mt. Sinai, tourists will be allowed in the resort areas of the country. Within hours of the announcement to open up the country, a tour company announced it would begin taking people to Mt. Sinai. It really is amazing that thirty-five years after Ron's discovery, the world will finally be able to see and walk where Moses walked.

Bibliography

Copyrighted materials used by permission of Jerry Bowen: https://www.anchorstone.com/newsletter-06-january-1994/.

Copyrighted materials used by permission of Jerry Bowen: https://www.anchorstone.com/newsletter-07-april-1994/.

Copyrighted materials used by permission of Jerry Bowen: http:www.anchorstone.com/newsletter-17-october-1994/.

Copyrighted materials used by permission of Kevin Fisher: https://www.arkdiscovery.com/joseph.htm/.

Copyrighted materials used by permission of Kevin Fisher: https://www.arkdiscovery.com/mt_sinai_found.htm.

Copyrighted materials used by permission of Kevin Fisher: https://www.arkdiscovery.com/red_sea_crossing.htm/.

Copyrighted materials used by permission of Anthony Grigor-Scott: https://www.biblebelievers.org.au/bb971126.htm/ Anthony Grigor-Scott.

Copyrighted article used by permission of CBN: Newshttps://www1.cbn.com/cbnnews/israel/2019/october/saudi-arabia-to-allow-access-to-ancient-biblical-sites-including-lsquo-the-real-rsquo-mount-sinai.

Copyrighted image used by permission of Kevin Gippert: CBS News Archives

Copyrighted materials used by permission of Aaron Sen: https://www.covenantkeepers.co.uk/red_sea.htm.

Copyrighted materials used by permission of Aaron Sen: https://www.covenantkeepers.co.uk/sinai.htm.

Copyrighted materials used by permission of Andrew Mark Jones htttp://www.discoveredsinai.com

Jewishencyclopedia.com.

Josephus, *Antiquities of the Jews*, Book II Chapter X.

Reprinted by permission of Gina Martin: https://news. nationalgeographic.com/2016/07/mosaic-synagogue-huq oq-israel-magness-archaeology/.

Copyrighted materials used by permission of Michelle Schelles: https://www.ronwyatt.com/red_sea_crossing.html (Newsletter 2, 1993).

Copyrighted materials used by permission of Michelle Schelles:https://www.ronwyatt.com/article_by_ron.html.

Copyrighted materials used by permission of Garry Pryce: https:// truediscoveries.org/red-sea-crossing/web-page-no-author.

https://www.amazon.com/Arabic-English-Dictionary-Modern English/087950003.

Salvation Prayer

Lord Jesus, Son of the Almighty God,
I come to you, knowing that I am a sinner.
I try to be good and do the right thing.
But again and again I fail and fall short.
I come to you, Lord Jesus repentant and unclean.
I ask you to forgive my sins, which are many.
I give my life to you; take it and make me clean.
And I thank You that through your shed blood
On a cruel cross and through your resurrection,
I am forgiven and saved throughout all Eternity
To be with You Forever. Amen

Author Biography

A senior, Pocahontas Simpkins Schuck, within two months of her eightieth birthday has just written a book entitled, <u>God's Treasure Red Sea Crossing.</u> This project began eleven months ago when she had finished all her coursework to obtain her doctorate. She is quoted as saying. "This is undoubtedly one of the most challenging endeavors that I had ever attempted." In speaking to people about getting a doctorate, she learned a new title, ABD which stands for All But Dissertation. Writing this paper is so difficult that people who did indeed finish their coursework, but not the dissertation use this title.

Her biography begins as she entered college in June 1959, a few days after her graduation from high school. She started quickly because she wanted to graduate in three years instead of four. Having been enthralled by one of her Biology classes in high school, she decided this would be her major in college.

At college it wasn't long before she realized that she wanted a name change. An upperclassmen dormitory was named Pocahontas or Pokie for short. She adopted the new nickname Pokie. Having been at school all summer, she was an expert when the new freshmen came in September. She was helpful to the incoming students, and has always been very friendly and well liked. When class elections were held she was voted to be the President of the incoming Freshmen.

At Radford College (now University) her suitemates were identical twins. Marge & Myra were born in Glacier National Park in Montana since their dad was a park ranger. The twins talked a lot about the adventures of snow drifts over the windows and roof of their home and a grizzly bear that walked into the kitchen. These stories caught Pocahontas' interest and she decided that she would like to become a national park ranger at Glacier. And that she did during the summers of 1969 and 1970. It never occurred to her that in those days only men held jobs as park rangers. So when she was hired at Glacier, she was told to buy a dark green pants suit because the park did not have one to give her. They did, however, order her a blouse and a pill-box hat from the dark green Delta-style uniform that had been designed for the few females across the United States holding the position as a national park ranger.

Some people have quoted the percentage of female rangers to be .025% at that time; one source cited thirteen female rangers in the entire United States. The uniforms included a skirt that was worn with high heel shoes & hose. This attire was not at all appropriate for the weekly hikes she led which included up to 30 visitors. The destination was an overnight stay at the Granite Park Chalet, an eight mile hike over rocky terrain. Her footwear had to be sturdy hiking boots. The other duties she performed at Glacier were: slide-show talks at St. Mary Visitor Center, campfire talks at Rising Sun Campground, guided boat tours on the beautiful St. Mary Lake, and she also worked the desk at the Logan Pass and St. Mary Visitor Centers.

The position as ranger was seasonal (during the summer) due to the fact that Pocahontas had a full time career as a science teacher in the public schools. Throughout the 1960s she taught in VA, and SC. During the 68-69 school year she held the position of science supervisor for Richland County School District #2 in

SC. After beginning her second career in Montana, she worked in other National Parks. During the fall of 1969 and the spring of 1970 she worked on the Blue Ridge Parkway at Humpback Rocks Visitor Center on weekends as she pursued her Masters degree at the University of Virginia.

The following summer, 1970 she returned to Glacier and worked on the West side of the park near Lake McDonald. For the first two weeks of the season it rained every day; hardy park visitors always showed up to take a four mile round trip hike that she led to Avalanche Lake. She was thrilled when the two weeks were over and there was blue sky on the horizon. Another duty she performed was giving evening slide presentations to over four hundred park visitors.

During the summer of 1971 she was hired at Richmond Battlefield Park as the first woman ranger and the first naturalist to hold that position. Her uniform for this position had been designed and adopted the previous summer. The uniform was beige and white and made of polyester fabric. The choices to wear for work were a tunic, slacks, culottes, and a dress. This uniform also included a flat-hat stetson and white boots. Her duties involved working with the Richmond Department of Recreation and Parks to set up a SumFun program for inner city youth. For a change of pace during the summer of 1972 she flew to Switzerland with a group of students on a summer snow skiing trip. She learned to ski for the first time at thirty-two years old.

Moving to the northeastern states for most of the 1970's & 80's she taught in New Jersey, Connecticut and Massachusetts. It was during these years that her daughter, Dawn & son, John were born. Returning to Virginia in 1991 she helped start a new school, Beville in Dale City (Woodbridge), Virginia. She taught at this school for fourteen years until her retirement in 2005 after spending forty-three years in the classroom. Upon her retirement from teaching science, she designed and built her retirement home facing Monroe Bay in Colonial Beach, Virginia. She presently resides there with her golden retriever, Sydney. Landscaping for the new home was a big project for her but she enjoyed every moment of it. Although most of it was accomplished in the cold weather of November and December.

While living in Woodbridge she worked at Great Falls Park, Virginia during the summer of 1992. This was the first ranger job where she wore the present female uniform (approved in 1978) which is the same as the uniform worn by men. Her duties included working the Visitor Center desk, leading hikes to the locks at Matildaville. These locks were George Washington's idea of a way to circumvent the falls on the Potomac River which is owned by the state of Maryland. A major portion of the position at this park was consumed with the Junior Ranger Program that she co-authored with another ranger. She and Nelson Hoffman won the Potomac Heritage Award of $5,000.00 for the park due to their design and implementation of the Junior Ranger Program.

During the summers of 93-95 she was a park ranger at Wolf Trap Park in Vienna, near D.C. The land where the park is located was donated in 1966 by Catherine Filene Shouse. The name Filene is well known; her family owned Filene's Basement in New York City. She also donated the funds to build the Filene Center for the performing arts. When I worked there Mrs. Shouse was still living and would drive herself in her Mercedes from her home on the other side of the Dulles Toll Road to the park. The ranger duties at this park were different than at any other national park area. These duties involved parking cars before the shows, also directing traffic before and after the shows. The most interesting part of this job was working 'the top of the circle' where she checked in famous stars and sent them backstage to park.

While still working at Wolf Trap during the summer of 1995 she and her daughter helped fill in at the President's Park (White House). Her duties at President's Park included working in the White House Visitor Center & the Ellipse Visitor Pavilion. She also helped distribute free tickets to visit the White House before 9/11. (After 9/11 tours were suspended for many months.) Monitoring the long lines of people who showed up for tickets was a challenge. Sometimes the lines were so long they would extend from the door of the White House Visitor Center around the entire block, which enclosed the Commerce Building, back to the entrance door. The people who had successfully obtained the tickets would gather at the appointed time written on the ticket. The gathering place for the tour groups was the bleachers near the Ellipse Visitor Pavilion. Another part of this position was to escort the waiting visitors to the SE Gate of the White House where they would go through the security building. Secret Service officers were in charge of the tours of the White House.

From 1995-2014 during the month of December she was assigned to work at the White House National Christmas Tree site. As an unofficial duty at this site, she helped keep the trains surrounding the large tree moving and on their tracks. Once she overheard a "wise guy" 4 year old explaining why Thomas the train couldn't run due to the fact that the coal car was in the rear as a caboose. She never confessed to being the perpetrator for that mis-match.

While she was working at the White House sometimes she filled in on the National Mall. She led tours and worked in the visitor centers of the Memorials at Jefferson, Lincoln, FDR, World War II and the Washington Monument. In those days the monument was open for night tours. She taught science during the day and worked as a ranger at the Washington Monument at night. During the years she worked as a park ranger in the D.C. area (1995-2012) she was invited to be a member of the Ranger Honor Guard. They marched in many parades including the Fourth of July, Cherry Blossom, and Presidential Inaugurations. There were also events at the Arlington Cemetery, funerals, opening of new park sites, and the Martin Luther King commemoration each year on January 15th.

As her last job with the National Park Services she spent seven years driving only fifteen miles to George Washington Birthplace National Monument. Although her college major had been in science, she quickly adapted to being in a historical park with all the farm animals: sheep, pigs, chickens, ducks, turkeys, cows and horses. She even had a friendly sheep named Houdini, that came to her when she called. In her interpretation role, she gravitated to the genealogy of the Washingtons. On special occasions she wore a period design gala gown for serving punch and giving her hourly talk at the Memorial House.

Upon her 2nd retirement, this time from the Department of the Interior, National Park Services, she received her Bachelor of Biblical Studies, Master of Divinity and finally her Doctor of Theology. Her dissertation was a seed planted for this book, God's Treasure Red Sea Crossing.

Photo by Walter Rabke

"Dr. Schuck presents real facts that bring to light truth about a mystery of ancient history. Utilizing her extensive teaching background and solid research she presents a factual and concise narrative of what really happened in The Red Sea Crossing. She makes the case for the true story in a way that is compelling, easy to follow and understandable. I highly recommend this book for all who seek truth. It should be added to every believers' library of tools for defending the faith."

--Fletcher Christiansen,
Industrial Planning Consultant

"I believed in the Red Sea Crossing based on faith. It was such a comfort to read the amazing details in God's Treasure Red Sea Crossing that substantiate, through historical and geographical research, the journey of Moses. Pokie transforms an age-old story into a journey founded in faith and fact."

--Veronica Foster, Author
Storybridges, Language Programs for Children

Endorsements:

"Wow! Great read. Nice pictures and maps. Well thought out text. I became immersed when starting, and finished the book in one sitting. Well researched, and lots of information in a great reading format. I was disappointed to have it end."

--James Wm. Donahue, D.D.S.0

"Dr. Pocahontas Schuck presents a new in depth book, <u>God's Treasure Red Sea Crossing</u>. Her new information exposes misconceptions of the true location of the real Mount Sinai; it will provide you with a different perspective of the centuries old mysteries. With the recent announcement of Saudi Arabia opening their borders to tourism the prospects of further exploration relating to this topic are now a reality. Dr. Schuck is definitely on the cutting edge of her hypothesis."

--Trish King,
Lay Speaker. Methodist Church

""Bernard W. Anderson in his book, <u>Understanding The Old Testament</u> wrote, "The Exodus was a Divine event. What happened was God's redemption of his people.". The location of the crossing of the Red Sea is carefully examined in this book. It is thought provoking and informative. The author has invested much time and effort to clarify many questions that biblical students have asked concerning various aspects of the exodus event. God's protection of His people is emphasized with the destruction of the Egyptian army."

--Paige A Young,
Pastor for 50 years

"This book, written by Dr. Pocahontas Schuck, was an eye opening adventure. The research for this project completely supported Dr. Schuck's opinion that history has identified the wrong site for Mt. Sinai. I must admit that when I started reading the material, it sent me straight to my Bible. For so long history has defined how we look at the events in the Bible; we have been told what interpretation we should believe. It was interesting that Dr. Schuck's research supports the discoveries made by Ron Wyatt who started finding proof of the wrong Biblical sites being identified. I also enjoyed how she wove descriptions of Bible people and their lives into the texts. Identifying the names helped by placing them there and making it easier to understand."

--**Rita Chandler**, retired veteran
Marine Corps and Army.

"Bravo Dr. Schuck for bringing light to this very important topic! Every human being, let alone every God-fearing believer, needs to know that real and tangible evidence of God's epic miracle does in fact exist. This easy to read book not only sets the record straight regarding the facts of the Red Sea Crossing, but also with regard to those brave souls who worked tirelessly to find the evidence despite immense opposition. Thank you Dr. Schuck for lending your time, talents and voice to glorify God and educate the rest of us."

Teresa C. Young

NOTES

NOTES

NOTES

NOTES

NOTES

NOTES

NOTES

NOTES